NO PAIN,
NO GAINES

NO PAIN, NO GAINES

THE GOOD STUFF DOESN'T COME EASY

CHIP GAINES

W Publishing Group

An Imprint of Thomas Nelson

No Pain, No Gaines

© 2021 Chip Gaines

All rights reserved. No portion of this book may be reproduced, stored in a retrieval system, or transmitted in any form or by any means—electronic, mechanical, photocopy, recording, scanning, or other—except for brief quotations in critical reviews or articles, without the prior written permission of the publisher.

Published in Nashville, Tennessee, by W Publishing, an imprint of Thomas Nelson.

Thomas Nelson titles may be purchased in bulk for educational, business, fundraising, or sales promotional use. For information, please email SpecialMarkets@ThomasNelson.com.

Any internet addresses, phone numbers, or company or product information printed in this book are offered as a resource and are not intended in any way to be or to imply an endorsement by Thomas Nelson, nor does Thomas Nelson vouch for the existence, content, or services of these sites, phone numbers, companies, or products beyond the life of this book.

This is a work of nonfiction. The events and experiences detailed herein are all true and have been faithfully rendered as remembered by the author, to the best of his ability. Some names have been changed to protect the privacy of the individuals involved.

Cover photo by Mike Davello. Interior illustrations by Mary Grace Greene.

ISBN 978-0-7852-3794-5 (audiobook)
ISBN 978-0-7852-3793-8 (eBook)
ISBN 978-0-7852-3791-4 (HC)
ISBN 978-0-7852-5361-7 (ITPE)

Library of Congress Cataloging-in-Publication Data
Library of Congress Control Number: 2020952509

Printed in the United States of America
21 22 23 24 25 LSC 10 9 8 7 6 5 4 3 2 1

My life has been shaped by the people in my network. People who say yes to life, yes to hard work, and yes to risk, but who aren't yes-people. People who have fought for me and beside me as I have for them. People who I trust with all my heart and who trust me with theirs.

This book is for them.

To Jo. Win or lose, it's always you and me forever.

To our kids, Drake, Ella, Duke, Emmie Kay, and Crew. You five are daily reminders of all that is possible in this world when we live and love and trust one another with everything in us.

To my parents and sister and Jo's parents and sisters. You were our earliest networks and our first cheerleaders. You have shaped and continue to shape us into the people we are.

To everyone else who has come alongside me over the years. Who has taught me what it looks like to expect greater for myself and to seek the extraordinary. Who has extended kindness to me even when it's been uncomfortable. Who has been willing to bet on me and shown me the reward that comes with being willing to bet on other people.

You all are a part of my network, and I wouldn't be who I am without each of you.

CONTENTS

FOREWORD

Thinking of times Chip has done things differently isn't hard. When I sat down to write this chapter, I thought I knew exactly what I'd say. I figured I could talk about the countless times I've watched him close a deal with a handshake when it might've been safer to sign a contract. Or the times he has hired on a few guys just to help them get on their feet. I thought I'd tell you all about how, for as long as I've known him, he's been a serial business card collector. Early on in our relationship, we'd be out at dinner and he'd end up talking with the owner, asking him questions about turnover and operating costs, and we'd walk out of the restaurant with the proprietor's card. He'd run into a painter at the hardware store and add another card to the collection. One time, I watched him exchange cards with a stranger he'd struck up a conversation with while pumping gas. Apparently, the guy knew how to lay tile. It's been nearly twenty years of life together and those business cards continue to fill the big black binder stowed beneath the front seat of Chip's truck. They're every bit a part of his daily rhythm as his well-worn drive into town.

One day a few years ago, as Chip hopped back in the truck from what was supposed to be a "quick errand" and filed away yet another business card, I asked him about it. "You never know when we may need it," he'd said. I sat there thinking, *I don't know anyone who needs the number to six different plumbers.* Chip and I saw the value of those cards differently. I'd always thought of business cards as a means to an end. But Chip saw them as a beginning. A potential connection worth having and holding on to.

In a way, that says it all. To Chip, those cards carry a currency far more valuable than what there is to gain from the information printed on them. They represent connections he's made with people he's met along the way whose lives have become stitched together with his simply because he chose to say hello, to ask what they do and what they care about. Simply because he was open to seeing them not for who they are in relation to him but for who they are all on their own.

The thing I've realized about Chip is that it's never really been about *how* he does anything—*how* he networks, *how* he does business, *how* he connects with people. He has never set out to do things differently. He is the thing that's different. Because for Chip, it's always been about the *why*.

Whether someone looks and acts and talks like Chip, or is different in every seemingly possible way, when he engages with them it's not with the intent to reinforce who he has always been but to sharpen who he is still becoming. As much in our life as in our business, Chip is always looking for ways to move forward. He never wants to be stuck. He's never content with the status quo or the way things have always been done. Growth is the measure of his life. That's his *why*.

This feels especially important at this moment. Never in my lifetime have I felt such a dissonance in our country. I've watched as our culture has made it acceptable to mute people or unfollow those who aren't like them. People who challenge their thinking, who call them out before they're ready. Social media has offered the convenience of making new connections but just as quickly shows how fragile those relationships were to begin with if they fracture when faced with a difference in perspective.

Chip just does not operate this way. He genuinely desires to understand and learn from those around him. He seeks out opportunities to interact with someone who is different from him. To ask questions and then be willing to answer questions in return. He wants to be challenged if there's a chance for growth and a chance to build something better. Something real.

I get that we all have different comfort levels when it comes to putting ourselves out there. Chip is a born connector. And me? I am naturally wired to be more reserved. But what I've realized is that it's more our insecurities than anything else that hold us back from taking a chance and trusting someone new. And what I've learned watching Chip engage with people is that when we can push whatever fears we carry to the periphery—whether it's a fear of not fitting in, of getting burned, of being wrong—it's with renewed clarity that we can see the beauty of what other people bring to the world and, in turn, better appreciate what we have to offer.

A life in pursuit of growth isn't easy. Of course there have been times I've witnessed Chip's desire to engage get him sidelined. I've seen him be bulldozed when he's put himself out there. Yet he sees those moments of painful exposure as fleeting, and they've never stopped him from getting up, scraping himself off, and trying again. Chip dares greatly, and he dares often. He has shown me the reward that comes with a willingness to dig in, to raise my voice for whatever passion might be buried deep within me, to be open to being challenged, and to kindly challenge others. Because when you get to the other side of a reckoning like that, you're a stronger and more gracious human for having gone through it.

Chip's heart and intention for connection have naturally formed this community of people whom he trusts and who, in turn, trust him. People whom he's given a chance to and who have offered him that same chance. Call it a network, a community, a home team. These people have come alongside us in the good times as often as in the bad. These are the people who tell us how it is and expect us to do the same. Whom we know we can count on and who know they can count on us.

This is something Chip deeply wants for everyone. It's why he wrote this book. And it's what makes it a love story, *Chip style*. Because it will challenge your perspective. It will make you question your fears. It will cause you to ask yourself what is keeping you from living a life of rich, authentic connection. But it will also remind you of all that is sacred in who you already are and of your extraordinary uniqueness. And it will ask you to share those parts of yourself with a world that's desperate to know them.

I am grateful every day to catch a glimpse of the world through Chip's eyes. He reminds me what life can look like when you're willing to believe with complete abandon that we are all made better when we trust one another and work together. It's a shift in perspective that costs me nothing yet colors the world in a much brighter, better hue. And that view, well, I wouldn't trade it for anything.

—Joanna Gaines

ACKNOWLEDGMENTS

My name might be on the cover of this thing, but no book is built by just one person. Without these creative minds, this idea I had one morning about how we build our network of people wouldn't exist as anything more than a few thoughts scratched onto a piece of paper. This group of people brought those ideas to life and helped me build them into something I hope they are as proud of as I am.

Kaila Luna, what can I say that would suffice? Steady from start to finish. Through not only these crazy times but also through the birth of your first beautiful baby. All the things, all the crazy twists and turns.. and yet there you always were. Listening and writing. Thank you.

Becky Cole, you brought your wit and wisdom to this project, and I'm grateful. Thank you for the good conversation.. and for never interrupting my stories (even the ones I'd already told you!).

Alissa Neely, you're like a little sister to me. Thank you for keeping this whole project on schedule. Without you, we wouldn't have released this book until 2029.

Kelsie Monsen, for your killer design skills, and for making me and this book look good.

Heidi Spring, thank you for all the tireless behind-the-scenes work you did on this project.

Uncle Ricky; Gabe and Justin Grunewald; Chip Smith; Brian Campion; Dr. Tanner; my granddad, J.B.; and, of course, my mom and dad, for showing me a way of life that woke me up and got me moving toward a future I could be proud of, and for allowing me to share each of your extraordinary stories in this book.

CHAPTER 1

NO PAIN, NO GAINES

I believe in sweat equity. By that I mean actual physical labor. The kind that makes you ache with exhaustion yet fills you with pride the moment your head finally hits the pillow. I always have. It was just one of those things that was built into my DNA.

When I was just a kid struggling to engage in school, it was how I set myself apart. Maybe I wasn't destined to be valedictorian, but I always knew I could rely on my ability to work harder than anyone else.

From an early age, I spent countless summers working out the nuances of every sport imaginable. I pounded the pavement selling books door to door till late into the evening. I trimmed trees and mowed acres of grass from dawn till dusk in the scalding Texas sun. Now I restore hundred-year-old houses back to their former glory. I build new houses from scratch. Perspiration and aching muscles make me feel alive. If I come home at the end of the day and my shirt and boots are clean, I don't feel right. I feel unsettled, like I've shorted myself somehow. But when I've physically worked hard, when I've given something of myself and can actually *feel* what it cost me, that to me is time well spent. Those days hold real worth.

I remember one time back when I was a sophomore in high school, my granddad, J.B., took me out to his ranch to help him dig some post-holes for a fence he planned to build. J.B. had another errand to run, so he dropped me off and told me to get to work until he came back around lunchtime.

I'm a very competitive person, always trying to prove myself. I got that from my dad. In our house, when the mail came, it was a race to see who could get back with it first. If you ordered a pizza, it was a competition to see who could eat it the fastest. J.B. was always messing with me about being a city boy, so when he left me there, I thought, *I'll show him. I'm gonna go dig some holes.*

If you've ever seen a posthole digger, it's not a real comfortable tool to use. You've got a shovel handle on your right and you've got a shovel handle on your left, and at the bottom two thin shovel heads come together. When you stab it into the dirt, you pull these two handles apart and it closes the two shovels together. You pick up some earth and drop it right next to where you dug it up. Doesn't sound like much, 'cause you're not having to move the dirt twenty-five feet; you're just moving it a couple of inches. You pick up dirt, you drop it. You do that until you get down about a foot and a half. Then, due to the nature of those thin shovel heads, you have a hole about six to eight inches in circumference.

I got to it, and right away I realized that the dirt seemed more like concrete. *No big deal*, I thought. *This requires no critical thinking, no strategy. It's just a lot of hard work. I know how to do* that.

So I kept at it, and by hole number four, my arms were burning. The dirt I was digging into was rock-solid earth. By five, I could feel the blisters forming on my hands and realized this was going to be a looong several hours. The force of that posthole digger hitting that rock-hard dirt made those blisters throb until they finally burst. And once the blisters burst, it was like I was not only tunneling through solid concrete inch by inch but doing so while holding a scalding-hot tool with my hands on fire. The more I worked and clawed at those holes, the slower I felt I was going, and the less it seemed I was accomplishing.

I held my head up to look down at the long row of holes left to dig. I wasn't more than an hour into this thing. Before I'd started, I thought I would have dug twelve or fifteen by now.

I was down on my hands and knees for like fifteen minutes trying to catch my breath, a little frustrated and a *lot* embarrassed. What had I gotten myself into? I still had a couple more hours until J.B. returned, so I stood up and lugged myself back over to the next post. There might've been a few tears in my eyes.

When J.B.'s truck appeared I got a little flushed in the cheeks. I'd managed to dig only ten holes since he'd dropped me off that morning.

What do you know—he hopped out of his truck, walked over to me, and told me what a hell of a job I'd done. I hadn't given up, and for that he was proud of me. Through my blisters and through my aching muscles, it was evident that I had given it my all.

It may not have looked like a job well done to me, but J.B. could see that. Despite the embarrassing number of holes, the evidence of my hard work was actually found in my effort. I might've been knocked down a peg or two, but you know what? That night I went to bed proud and woke up the next day ready to do it again.

It's like I told you—I like to sweat. That's been true ever since I was a little pint-sized hustler selling candy and Capri Suns down at the public tennis courts or doing yard work with my parents. Later, I sweat plenty running circles out on the baseball field and putting in long hours starting various small businesses. You've probably even seen me sweat when Joanna and I did *Fixer Upper.* I've got no shame about any of that. I didn't bat an eyelash telling you about how digging posts nearly did me in. I'm proud of it. I have always known deep in my bones that hard work yields great results, even when there's little evidence of it.

Joanna and I have built our entire lives around this notion. We've put decades of hard work and grit and a whole lot of sweat equity into the work we do, and now we're launching into what might be the hardest work we've ever done: building a network. We were a few months out from our launch date when I realized—and I swear it was as crystal clear as I'm telling you now—that this physical network we are building wouldn't be possible without the network of people who have poured their lives into both me and Joanna and the work we're doing. Some when we were young, and some laboring alongside us now. I told Jo, "I think I want to write a book about how we've built our network."

Jo and a few people on our publishing team kindly pointed out that there are already a lot of books out there about networking, and I would add that most of them were probably written by people much smarter than I am. Books that I'm sure have a ton of extremely useful tips in them, but most of those books focus on *how* to network, "network" the verb. How to go out into the world and meet powerful people who can turbocharge your career. But that's not at all what I'm after, and not at all what you'll find in this book. I am more interested in "network" the *noun*, the group of people with beating hearts and passions who live and love and try and fail, and who are there beside you as you do the same.

Hard work yields great results, even when there's little evidence of it. #makesense

The title of this book was going to be *Building a Network* because I'm a sucker for wordplay (get it—building a network?). But I kept veering off track. Every time I started thinking about my own network of people, I'd think about the circumstance that bonded us. It certainly wasn't any kind of "networking" event.

My network has been built by a bunch of small moments. Moments where someone extended me kindness instead of anger, and I chose to pay that kindness forward. Moments when someone told me, "It's just business," and I refused to believe them. Moments when I had their backs and they had mine, even when it looked inevitable that we were going to lose. Moments I chose to do right by someone or they chose to do right by me, even when what was right was far from easy. Moments when either one of us could have brushed the other off because it wasn't convenient, but we didn't. Moments when we chose to lean in instead of pulling apart. Moments when authentic human connection was more important than any other earthly thing, when we decided to bet on each other instead of the way of the world.

Those experiences required hard work. It was painful at times. But boy was it worth it! And it got me thinking about what those fleeting moments of discomfort, inconvenience, and pain have yielded over a lifetime—a network of people I trust and who trust me.

In Jo's and my life, these are people so outstanding they have come through for us in good times and bad. People who remind us who we are and what we value and don't let us settle for anything less. People who have our confidence because they can be counted on no matter what. People who have lifted us up and who know that we will do the same for them.

A network like this doesn't come easy. To say it requires sweat equity would be an understatement. It requires faith in people. It requires trust. It requires hope and lots and lots of very hard work. Not necessarily the kind of work that makes your back ache or hands throb, but equally hard, fulfilling work. Because sometimes you can be surrounded by people and yet still feel utterly alone. But you work to find one person you can lean on—that's one connection. You work to find someone else who believes in who you are, not what you can do for them—that's another connection. Before long, you've got a series of connections that hold you up. And this work, when done, can yield a network that can sustain you for a lifetime. A network like the fence I was building at my granddad's ranch. A single post may not be worth much, and building it was *painful*, but connect it to another post, and then another, and what you've *gained* is something strong, something reliable, something that can shape the world.

BOTTOM LINE

You get what you work for.

CHAPTER 2

BLUE CHIP

I had this amazing poster when I was a kid, maybe ten or so. It was a photograph of a mansion perched on a hilltop high above the ocean. Silhouetted against a neon-colored sunset, the house was surrounded by palm trees, and it obviously cost a fortune. But the mansion wasn't the focus of the shot. That honor went to a five-bay garage holding five different luxury sports cars, each one fancier than the last. The caption read, "Justification for higher education." And I believed it. A Ferrari, a Lamborghini, a Porsche, a Maserati, a Corvette, and a big house on a hill—what better way to show the world that you made it.

I used to lie in bed and fantasize about what it would be like to go out to that garage and have my pick of cars and then.. and then.. well, I have to admit that's pretty much where the fantasy stopped. I didn't spend much time thinking about what I would do once I got that stuff. It seemed like enough to me just to get it.

The thing was, I'd drunk the Kool-Aid. That specialty drink that society whips up for us that tells us that the way to quench our thirst is to acquire things—status, fancy objects, a high-powered job. It wasn't all that appealing to me. I wasn't even sure I liked that Kool-Aid, but from what I could tell, it was the drink of choice for a lot of the adults around me.

My dad, who came from next to nothing, worked his tail off to provide a life for us where we had everything we needed. Over the course of his career, he had met a few people who seemed to be headed straight for a mansion on a hill. Looking back, they weren't but one or two rungs above him on the corporate ladder, but Dad and I thought they had it all figured out. Most of them belonged to the local country club, an imposing building on sprawling grounds where impossibly green grass spread like a welcome mat under their soft-soled shoes.

Every once in a while, one of these guys would invite us to spend the day at the club. You might think I ran straight for my bathing suit and sunscreen, but instead of grabbing my Walkman and my trunks, I grabbed a notebook and a pen. You see, I was on a mission to find out what it took to get to that promised land myself. I would tell my friends to go ahead to the pool; I'd meet them there. Meanwhile, I'd lurk around the clubhouse watching the crowd, and as soon as one of the alphas separated from the herd, I would be there in front of him with my little notebook, eyes bright as pennies, saying, "Hi there, sir. My name is Chip Gaines. Do you mind if I ask you a few questions?" Half of them probably thought I was a reporter for the school newspaper, but most of them humored me.

I'd start in with my questions, asking them how they got to where they were in life. The answers they gave wouldn't surprise you at all. In fact, you could probably write a Mad Lib that would do the trick. "I went to [insert Ivy League school here], where I majored in [choose one: law, business, finance, medicine]. After graduation I got a job at [national corporation]." I'd dutifully scribble all that down, and then

I'd ask my *real* question: "Tell me about your passion and purpose—that thing that kept you up at night and drove you when things were really tough."

They'd look at me, eyebrows cocked, and say, "What do you mean passion and purpose? I found a good job. Solid. Reliable. Safe. Look where it got me."

Surely they hadn't understood. I'd try asking ten more ways. But the response was always the same: "This is *the* path, kid. It's worked for me and it's worked for that guy over there and that lady over there too. If you want all this, trust us; it'll work for you." They never said a word about passion or purpose or things like changing the world. They thought I only wanted to know how to get to the country club. As a kid I was confused. *Wait, I thought the way to the country club equaled passion, purpose, and a chance to change the world.*

The country-club set turned out to have what I think of as a brass-ring problem. You know the expression "grab the brass ring"? It's a reference to old-fashioned merry-go-rounds that used to have a brass ring on a pole that you could try to grab as you went 'round and 'round. The goal was to be the first person to grab it. But the problem is, if you are so focused on grabbing the ring, you miss out on everything else going on—the music and family and friends and wild rides that twist and turn in every direction. The very stuff that makes the merry-go-round worth riding in the first place. The guys I interviewed all held the proverbial brass rings in their hands, but I wondered if they might have missed out on the stuff that makes life worth living and loving. I started to realize that if I followed that path, I was going to end up holding that same brass ring in my hands thinking, *I traded my ride for this?*

I'd thought these guys had the secret to the universe. I thought they'd be able to steer me toward a life of passion and success, but now they were telling me I would have to choose—it's one or the other. But what if I wanted both? If these folks, who had up until that point seemed to me the very epitome of success, couldn't help me find my way with passion, then who could?

These weren't bad people. In fact, most of them were good family men and leaders in their community. They just weren't ready to answer a question about the point of life from an eager kid who wasn't even old enough to vote. They were well-equipped to tell me how to get the stuff on that poster, but not so much how to quench that burning question, How can I make my life matter?

The more I looked at that stupid poster, the more I realized that I wasn't the only one who had been lied to. The people I'd looked up to had been lied to as well. We'd been made to believe that the stuff on that poster followed purpose and meaning. I believed that "stuff" equaled a life that matters.

What had me rattled was how unanimous their responses were. I couldn't find a single guy who looked me in the eye and said, "Let me tell you, kid, I wake up every day so alive, so inspired by what I do for a living, just aching to get at it, that I can't wait to see what the world brings me next. *That* is how I ended up here." It was like they'd all been turned out at the same factory. None of them seemed bothered by the fact that they weren't especially pumped about their lives because they'd looked around and seen that no one else seemed to be, either.

I'd heard the chestnut "You can judge a person by the company they keep." I'd always thought of it as a warning not to run with the wrong crowd—the fast kids who didn't seem to care much about morality or character or respect. But I started to think maybe there was another message there. Maybe that expression meant that you could tell a lot about how a person approached life by the network of people they surrounded themselves with. That threw me for a loop. I started to realize I wasn't going to be able to just plug in to the network that already existed around me. I was going to have to build one myself.

WHAT'S YOUR STATUS QUO STATUS?

As we get ready to figure this thing out together, let's get an idea of where your starting point is. Read the statements below and put a check mark next to the ones you agree with. Don't overthink it; just check off what feels right.

A

☐ The well-worn path is well worn for a reason: it's the proven way to succeed.

☐ If I stay in my lane, eventually I'll get where I'm going.

☐ Security is a prerequisite for happiness.

☐ If I can just get enough cash in the bank, I'll be set for life.

☐ I feel better today if I know what tomorrow is going to look like.

B

☐ There's a rush that comes from taking a risk.

☐ Failure is an old friend. I welcome it into my life.

☐ I look for moments of creativity, originality, passion, and purpose every day.

☐ Sometimes pursuing goals gets in the way of a good life.

☐ Going against the grain is the best way to gain traction.

If you checked more boxes in column B than column A, I hope this book inspires you to get out there and kick some butt. If you checked more boxes in column A than column B, I'm going to ask you to keep an open mind as I show you why I want to challenge some of that thinking. I hope by the end of it, your heart will be pumping a little harder.

As I've built my own network, I've discovered it isn't always easy to find the people who had my back—the ones who trusted me to do things I knew I had to do, even when half the time "what I had to do" sounded an awful lot like "having a screw or two loose." These are the people who believed in me to take risks, to fail, and then to fail again better the next time. People who, when we got to the equivalent of the top of the Empire State Building, didn't flinch when I admired the view for a minute and then said, "Now let's build a bigger building." But those people are out there. You just need to know what you're looking for.

There's a chorus of people who yak at you all day long about the virtues of a 401(k) and a steady day job and a fully funded retirement plan, and their voices can make it hard for you to hear your own over theirs. I certainly understand why people listen to that crowd. That crowd is *loud*. But as Ralph Waldo Emerson said, "None of us will ever accomplish anything excellent or commanding except when he listens to this whisper which is heard by him alone."[1]

I'm here to tell you, the whisper is there. You've just got to listen for it.

I believe that we've all got something to offer this world, every day, every hour, every minute. If we can surround ourselves with people who amplify that message instead of muffling it, we can turn that whisper into a roar.

That is what had gotten under my skin about those guys at the country club. They hadn't been able to hear that whisper over the crowd chanting. It was like they were following the crowd so closely they ended up living somebody else's life. Too often we suppress our own unique desires because what we want isn't "wise," or "you can't make a living at it." Or we get hung up on figuring out what our passions or purposes are in the first place and forget to ever get started.

Back in the day, it wasn't as common for people to go out in search of their passions. If you were born to a farmer, then your passion better be farming. You'd get up each morning and make your way out to the barn to milk the goats not because you had a fire in your soul to do so, but because doing so meant the survival of your family. It wasn't a complicated thing. You didn't have to beg your parents for $10,000 so that you could go and backpack around Europe in your flip-flops to figure out whether you were destined to squeeze goat udders or not. You just did it.

But at some point we evolved away from that. Suddenly we had so many options. Suddenly we had choices. If you want, you can become a doctor, a lawyer, a programmer, a carpenter, a designer, an exterminator, an engineer, a contractor, a teacher, a blogger, or about six million other things. Options are great! But infinite options can be paralyzing. It's like we have a hangover from the old days and we're expecting someone to come along and tell us which path to take. We still haven't found a way to determine our passions outside of the expectations of our family and society. A new set of expectations has supplanted the old ways. Instead of

becoming a farmer because that's what your family had done for genera-
tions, you chased a set of goals everyone seemed to agree were worth
chasing—without ever considering why you're doing it or figuring out
who or what it was that made you change course in the first place.

We all yearn for wise counsel, and there's nothing wrong with that.
Wisdom from those you trust can lead you in the right direction. But the
path you choose for yourself will take you the farthest.

**Wisdom from those you trust can lead you in the right direction. But the
path you choose for yourself will take you the farthest. #makesense**

REDEFINE "NETWORK"

When I reason out why I am able to act in accordance with that internal
whisper Emerson was talking about, it's not my ability to make some
harebrained idea I had come to fruition, or my to-the-bone work ethic,
or even my wit and charm. Bottom line, I owe my life's success to the
people whose own lives are stitched closely together with mine, who
either encouraged me to follow that inner whisper or whose own inner
whisper was eerily similar to mine. These are the people who make up
my network. In this book I'm going to tell you how to build a network of
your own—one that will make your life richer than you've ever imagined.

I want you to find your own blue-chip network. Let me explain
what I mean by that. I think of a blue-chip network like this: Back in
the 1920s people started using the term "blue chip" to refer to stocks
that are especially valuable—stocks in companies that are Grade A, top-
notch, reliable, and consistently profitable. Companies that stand the
test of time. They tend to share the same qualities: a visionary founder,
adaptability, stable leadership. Over time, the term was used to indicate something exceptionally worthwhile. A blue-chip athlete is a great

prospect. A blue-chip art gallery sells work that will hold value despite the whims of the market.

I want to expand that list to include a blue-chip *network*. A group of people so outstanding that they will come through for you in good times and bad. People who earn your confidence because they can be counted on no matter what. People who might not be common, but who are incalculably valuable.

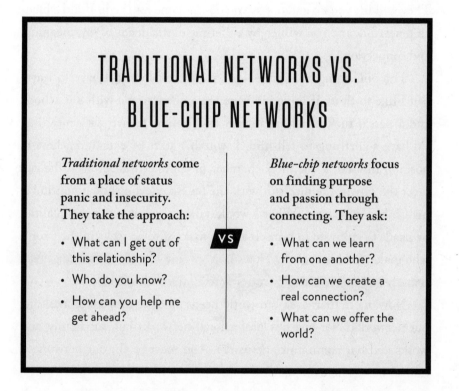

TRADITIONAL NETWORKS VS. BLUE-CHIP NETWORKS

Traditional networks come from a place of status panic and insecurity. They take the approach:	*Blue-chip networks* focus on finding purpose and passion through connecting. They ask:
• What can I get out of this relationship? • Who do you know? • How can you help me get ahead?	• What can we learn from one another? • How can we create a real connection? • What can we offer the world?

VS

We've all got a network, including you. Today it might include your family, your community, the people you work with. But if you want to extend that network to be one that will help you beat the odds, a blue-chip network, if you will, you'll want to be intentional about choosing the people in it. They're easy to spot if you know what to look for. They're radical connectors who see both our common core and what makes us different. They're people who are comfortable being uncomfortably kind. They're people with a fixer-upper mentality. People who know how to build mutual trust. People who make risk-taking their default setting. People who bring their experience, not their expectations, to all they do. People who are exceptional in character. People who are relational, not transactional. People who make authenticity nonnegotiable. People who are awake to life, not asleep at the wheel. People who act with intention. They will lift you up and out as you do the same for them. Build a blue-chip network and you will enjoy a lifetime of dividends of joy, meaning, and connection.

The only thing I know for sure is how much I still have to learn. But I like to think if some kid were to come up to me with a notebook and a pencil tucked behind his ear asking how to live with meaning, I'd have something to tell him. I wouldn't start by explaining how to position himself at the local chamber of commerce meeting so he can meet the guy in the nice suit with the fat Rolodex, or how to optimize his LinkedIn account. What I would talk to him about is the qualities he needs to cultivate in himself and to make sure he seeks in the people who make up his network. That's how you build a life of meaning. And that's pretty much what you're going to find in this book.

Now, more than ever, our world needs all of us to work on building our networks. Not just our professional networks but our family networks and our community networks. And most of all, our network as human beings here on planet Earth.

I've been building a network my whole life, from my earliest unlikely mentors to Joanna Gaines, the woman who is my partner in everything I do.

But it's our families who shape us most, so it occurred to me that it might be a good idea to let you hear from mine. (If nothing else, it'll give you a break from me for a page or three.) So I've included a couple of chapters called "My Network" that give their take on things.

Pieces of my history that influenced how I've gone about building my network.

There's a good chance that bookstores will shelve this book in the business category. Even though I have made my work central in my life, I cringe when someone says, "It's just business." I don't believe that. The decisions we make about how to approach our lives, including our careers, are anything but just business. Not when they impact our families, our friends, their hopes and dreams. It's never just business. If it costs you everything to become successful or to get your name on the side of some building somewhere, where does that leave you in the end? Alone and empty, holding a cheap brass ring with no one to share the fruits of your labor.

That's why I'd tell that hypothetical kid with a notebook that the ride is the thing—our one unpredictable, irreplaceable life that is ours and ours alone to live wildly, freely, uniquely as ourselves. *That's* the goal. That's what we should be reaching for.

Jo and I have a set of guiding lights that we publish in every issue of our magazine. These are precepts that keep us true, with none more important than this: "Of all heroic pursuits large or small, there may be none greater than a life well loved."

I'm telling you, that's *it*! That's the whole point of the ride. Love the life you've got, and live it well.

You may have heard the expression "You don't choose books; books choose you." I don't know what twist of fate brought this book into your hands, but now you're here. So let's do this. Let's start a movement, a network of people enlivened and electrified by the power of living according to their purposes, so that when someone looks around for examples to lead their way, *we'll* be the crowd saying, "Listen to your whisper, follow your own path."

I never did get one of those cars on the poster I had hanging in my bedroom as a kid. Frankly, you're a whole lot more likely to see me on a

John Deere tractor than squished in a Porsche. With a little life under my belt, I can see that poster was all kinds of wrong for me—and so was the country club. The house, the fancy cars, that lifestyle represented the end of a journey, a goal accomplished, boxes checked. Where's the fun in that? I didn't realize back then that the man I would grow up to be would have gotten to the top of that hill and walked right past those cars to look over the edge of the cliff to see what was next on the horizon—or that I would become a person who would rather spend an afternoon digging a hole for a fence post with my kid than having a gin and tonic at the nineteenth hole.

If I could go back in time and hang a new poster on the wall of my childhood bedroom, it would be a picture of me in my boots and jeans walking to the house after a long hard day's work, toward my family, heart full of passion and purpose. That, to me, is a life well loved.

BOTTOM LINE

When you focus only on "status," you end up with the status quo.

CHAPTER 3

NONNEGOTIABLES

I spent a decent portion of my life as an imposter, taking my cue from others about who I should be. It sounds bad, but I was *good* at it. I was good at fitting in, good at seeming like I belonged no matter what the scene. It helped that I loved to tell stories. Not just any old anecdote. Heroic fables and grand tales, most with only a grain of truth in them. Somewhere along the way I started to apply my storytelling skills to my own life. I'd hold my audience enthralled, telling them things like "I live in a mansion with a fleet of fancy cars" or "My dad is a professional football player who tackled some of the greatest players in the sport."

You might consider my stretching the truth like that to be a cry for attention, and it probably was. But the way I remember it is that the thrill of storytelling—the way other kids' eyes would get real big when I'd reveal something they didn't expect, and the questions they'd ask when they couldn't wait to know more—made me feel connected with people. I was tapping into a part of who I was at my core, even if in some cases it was built on something entirely make-believe. Wrap your head around *that*. I had used something authentically me—a natural ability to connect with and captivate people—to build a false front.

It took me a while, but I came to realize something important about what in life is nonnegotiable, what we can't be willing to concede—something you'll need to do if you're going to build a strong network.

Here's how I got there.

My dad named me after the main character in the Chip Hilton books. The series was written by Hall of Fame basketball coach Clair Bee, so, unsurprisingly, the stories were about sports. They had titles like *A Pass and a Prayer* and *Hoop Crazy*. Chip Hilton was an all-American stud. When people romanticize the 1950s, this kid is who they're thinking of—nice boy, loved his mama, good at sports, polite, just about every wholesome thing you can imagine. The way I was raised, I always identified with those values. That's who I was at heart. Still am.

When I was in third grade, we moved from Albuquerque, New Mexico, to a little town called Colleyville near Dallas. I never asked my parents why, but instead of moving right before school started, or the month after school ended, we moved in the middle of the school year. Actually, we moved right in the middle of the school week. Monday I was at school in Albuquerque and then Tuesday, I was in a different town, in a different school, with a bunch of kids going, "Who are you? Why is your name Chip? Why are you redheaded? Why do you have freckles?"

I realized pretty fast that I didn't have a lot of time to figure out how to fit in. These kids had already been together since kindergarten. So, chop-chop, when I met a new potential friend, whatever that kid needed me to be, I pretended to be that. I put myself through a master class of human observation, studying the other kids, trying to determine what they liked, what they were about.

The thing is, it worked. In sixth, seventh, and eighth grade, I was in the popular crew of kids who people wanted to be around. I didn't totally let go of that Chip Hilton kid I'd always been, but I learned how to shapeshift with the best of 'em, adopting the lingo, the laugh, the look of anyone I wanted to fit in with. I even wore boat shoes and tied a sweater around my neck one time, just to try to out-country-club the actual country club kids. I practiced shapeshifting all through high school.

Obviously there was a pretty significant insecurity hiding beneath those polo shirts. I started to believe that people were far more interested in their own version of me than the real me. So that's the one I tried to give them. All of them: the jocks, the band kids, the student council reps, the cowboys. One minute I was a cutup, if that's who you were looking for. The next I was ultracompetitive, if that was your deal. It was like a party trick: now you see me, now you don't.

As human beings we can get pretty creative about coming up with multiple personalities, taking cues from what other people seem to want. You look around to other people for evidence of who you should be. You laugh at something you don't think is that funny because other people are laughing at it. You pretend to like a band you hate or hate a band you love. You wear the sunglasses everyone else is wearing. These are small things, but it's death by a thousand papercuts to your sense of self. If you keep it up, it's easy to forget who you really are.

In high school I never veered *too* far from the real me, that Chip Hilton–esque kid. I went to the kind of high school where everybody was in one of the good-kid clubs. I didn't have a whole lot of friends who cut class, much less went out and got drunk and made fools of themselves. So the first party I went to when I got to junior college was quite the shock to my system. I rolled in with a couple of buddies, and as soon as I got through the door, there were multiple scenes playing out that I'd never imagined witnessing with my own eyes. Not long after I got there, this guy came up, slapped me on the back, and said, "Gaines, good to see you. What's up, you party animal? What are you drinking? Let me have a shot of that."

This was before Nalgene bottles, so I was carrying this Mason jar–looking thing with a lid. I had filled it with crushed ice and—what else would a Chip Hilton–type character fill this thing with?—orange juice. Yep. Fresh-squeezed was my drink of choice.

This guy grabbed my OJ and chug-a-lugged it, making this big obnoxious deal, *glug, glug, glug, glug, glug,* with a little bit running down both sides of his face. Finally, he passed it back to me and said, "Oh man. What's in that? Whew! Gaines is crazy, man!" And he just walked off.

For the first time since I was a kid back in Albuquerque, I was not *at all* tempted to shapeshift to fit into that scene. The girls pawing at me, some kid dragging himself across the floor because he's blackout drunk? That just didn't appeal to me.

I wrestled with my identity that whole year. I became a recluse. I *journaled*. I'd probably see it now and think, *What a clown.* But I took it really seriously. I was writing poems. I was out under a tree, drawing a freakin' landscape. I couldn't get my feet under me. Life was a constant negotiation between what other people seemed to think was the way to behave and how I felt inside. I really started to understand the expression "fish out of water." That was it. I was flopping around, 100 percent not in my element. The feeling was almost physical. I had to get out of there. It was not for me.

GET REAL REAL

When I transferred to Baylor the following year, I exhaled. These kids were more like the ones I'd known in high school, so it wasn't a minute till I was back to my old ways, charming, adapting, fitting in.

Before long, I'd gotten myself into a fix. In my first couple of weeks, I met a kid I'll call Peter. I can't remember what his parents did for work, but whatever it was, it allowed him to have $5,000 a month to spend on whatever he wanted. Not the necessities like books or courses or even the meal plan. I'm talking *five thousand extra dollars.*

I didn't want to run with Peter because of what he could do for me. I wanted to run with him so people would think that I was a high roller like he was. We went into this tit-for-tat thing, where I'd say, "Oh no, this round's on me" or "Hey, I've got this one." You don't have to be a mathematician to figure out that a couple hundred dollars in savings doesn't go far against $5,000 a month. One day I went to buy gas and my credit card was declined, and I realized I couldn't fake it to keep up with this kid. At least not for long. When I ran out of cash, I'd hide out for a few weeks until I could afford to go about with Peter again. It was a real shameful cycle.

You'd think that would have sent me a message, but my personality muscle had become so conditioned to create new identities that I continued to generate new versions of myself throughout college. I was still being the guy everybody liked because they'd think to themselves, *Hey, this guy is a lot like me!*

Fortunately, my imitation act took its final bow soon after I met Joanna Stevens. She didn't seem to want a made-to-order version of me. She saw through all that nonsense. After we'd been dating a while, Jo sat me down and told me she needed to know who it was she'd be marrying. It became clear how easily this charade could destroy my chance of a life with this woman. You can't sub in something artificial without compromising the integrity of the whole deal.

It was time to lock down a version of myself. It was not going to be Chip Gaines, High Roller, or Chip Gaines, Chameleon, or even Chip Gaines, All-American, but Chip Gaines, the Original. I might not have been buffed or polished, and I was really far from perfect, but I resolved to be perfectly real from then on.

Jo's question forced me to drop the act and take up the task of discovering who I really was. I had to peel back all those crappy layers

I'd accumulated and carried around with me since childhood so I could see what was really there from the beginning. Once I could clearly see the difference between what was fake and what was real, these qualities became my nonnegotiables: the strength of my faith, my dedication to my purpose, my love for my family, and my commitment to who I am. These were the watermarks that certified Chip Gaines, the Original. One of a kind, 100 percent unique. Every good thing in my life has come directly from my resolution to make these things nonnegotiable.

Identify your nonnegotiables, and all those made-up layers fall away. Then you start building from there. But peeling off layers you've worn for a long time is not easy. What you find underneath might be pretty unappealing at first—pale from the lack of exposure to sunlight, weak from lack of use. But ultimately you were given the stuff under there to hold you up and to help you move through the world. Once that outer protective layer is gone, and you get used to moving around without it, there's no feeling as beautiful and free.

WHAT ARE YOUR NONNEGOTIABLES?

Make a list of qualities that are an unwavering part of who you are. Next time you find yourself flopping around like a fish out of water, check that list. Are your actions in line with your nonnegotiables? Or, when you felt like you weren't acting like yourself, was it because you had compromised your nonnegotiables? What could you have done to change that?

I've managed to stay pretty true to my commitment to be Chip Gaines, the Original. When I've slipped up, I have paid the price.

Two years ago Jo and I learned that we had been included on *Time* magazine's Time 100 list. The list included people like LeBron James, the K-pop band BTS, Michelle Obama, and.. us. It took a minute for us to scrape ourselves off the floor when we got the news. We joked around like, *Are we being* Punk'd?

That night was like grown-up prom. Joanna wore a gorgeous dress, and I even put on a tie. This was a big-league event. From the moment we stepped out of the limousine, it was *Twilight Zone: Celebrity Edition*. Cameras, paparazzi, red carpet, the works. We kept saying to ourselves, *Holy cow, how are we qualified to be here?*

At one point, Taylor Swift came in. Now, there's famous, and then there's Taylor Swift. It was like she sucked all of the oxygen out of the room. While everyone was catching their breath, Taylor looked at Jo and what do you know, she made a little air heart in our direction. Jo and I turned and looked over our shoulders, like, "Gosh, I wonder who she's air-hearting." Someone had to poke Jo and say, "You, she's air-hearting *you*." I wanted to go over there and tell her, "Taylor, you know The Rock is here, right? If you want to air-heart somebody, it probably should be him! Or Nancy Pelosi. She's right over there." But it turned out she'd meant us.

At one point in the evening, a reporter asked us a few questions. Normally my inner voice is a real *rah-rah* guy saying to me, "You got this. Go on, you're about to make their heads spin." But when the interviewer asked me, "Chip, what art has influenced you and Joanna over the past six months?" my inner voice went stone-cold silent. *My* head spun. I was trying to think of the name of the guy who painted the *Mona Lisa* or the other guy who did the Sistine Chapel. Instead I came up with nothing. Nada. Zero. Zip. Zilch.

It was all over with by eleven or midnight. Afterward we didn't pop champagne or change out of one ensemble into another so we could go to the after-party. We went straight to our hotel like a pair of zombies.

In a fog, we sat on the bed and asked each other, "What just happened? Why do we feel like we just got kicked in the face?"

The light slowly came back into our eyes. We stayed up until two or three that morning dissecting why the night had felt so *off.* As we talked, Jo reminded me of another time I'd felt my world tilt on its axis like that.

A couple of years earlier we'd been filming an ad for one of our partnerships. Normally, no matter what the occasion, you'll find me in the same outfit: jeans, T-shirt, and boots. I've worn suits for weddings and for things like the gala where it would have been disrespectful not to, but nearly every other day of my adult life you will find me in jeans and a T-shirt. It's like my second skin. But for this shoot, the directors had me trussed up like a Christmas goose. I was wearing a black tux and sitting in a velvet chair by a fireplace with a shih tzu on my lap. There may have been a pipe involved. Or at least that's how I remember it. I felt ridiculous. It was Chip Gaines III, Esq.

I looked down at my lap and asked, "Whose dog is this?"

The directors told me, "That's your dog!"

Then I asked, "Whose fireplace is this?"

They must have thought I was joking around, 'cause no one answered. But this was no joke to me. People know us. They know we live on a farm. If they saw this ad and thought, *Wait a minute, that's not his house—or his dog,* how long before they started wondering what else wasn't real? Like, were those really my kids? Were Jo and I actually who we seemed? That shapeshifting feeling came back, and it felt like some serious black magic.

Assistants were buzzing around, getting light readings and checking sound, when all of a sudden, my heart started beating fast. I could hear the blood rushing in my ears. My skin felt itchy, my throat closed up, it got hard to breathe. It was like I was having an allergic reaction. *What the heck?* I excused myself to go to the restroom to pull myself together. That is literally what it felt like. I had to pull my *self* back into my own body.

After a few minutes, I got control and finished the promo, but I have to tell you, I was rattled.

Probably a dozen times since that moment I've had that same thing happen. The world kind of zooms in and out around me and I get dizzy. A bubble swells up in my chest, and something pushes down on it, making me feel like it could pop at any second. I have to take deep, gasping breaths, close my eyes, and say to the people around me, "Hold on one second. Sorry. Holy smokes. I kind of lost my breath there." I come up with some cute little comment like, "Boy, I'm half the man I used to be." Or I'll imply I did some physical activity that took it out of me, 'cause that's sure how it feels. But the fact is, the source isn't physical or mental; it's emotional.

I realized in that hotel room that every time my world takes a nosedive, I can trace it back to a single source: a dizzying gap between how I see myself and how the world is treating me. When I feel the pressure of a world that is trying to sway or dictate my behavior to make one of my nonnegotiables negotiable, it sends me for a tailspin.

When I was being interviewed at the *Time* event, that's what had happened: I'd let the idea of what that answer was supposed to look like get in the way of an answer that came from me, from my heart. I should have just laughed and said, "Man, I'm a construction guy from Waco, Texas. My idea of a work of art is a perfect three-bedroom house. If you're talking painting, you wanna see the one my kid did that we have hanging on the fridge?" I should have gone back to what defines me as a person, my values, my nonnegotiables. I don't care much about art or fancy parties or awards. I care that my kids think I'm a good dad. I care that I am a good husband to my wife. I care that my business is strong and that we are raising up and training leaders.

What leads us to believe that the original version of who we are isn't enough? Who was it in your life who convinced you that you needed layers of camouflage to be worthy of acceptance? What passing comment started out as a "note to self" but turned into a false identity?

Now consider the source of that comment. Was that person credible? Were they qualified to speak on behalf of your purpose? I doubt it. Yet here so many of us are, wrestling off those "fleeting" comments, wearing each one like a layer of armor. Ready for battle.

Each time we concede to someone else's opinion of us, or we willingly buy into some lesser truth or inaccurate picture of who we are, what we're really doing is surrendering our purpose. I believe with all my heart that when we abandon our true purpose, the thing God made us to do, we're not the only ones who suffer. There's a ripple effect. It really does change *everything* for *everyone*.

As much in business as in life, authenticity often means sticking with your gut in the midst of difference or even indifference. It goes hand in hand with discernment, an ability to "test the spirits" and see what is false. If you throw your thought or opinion out into the world and it comes back confirming your gut instinct, then you've got even more confidence to go and do that thing. But if the opposite happens, and it comes back smelling of uncertainty, then maybe it's time to heed the advice of those whose insight you trust.

Other times, being authentic is as simple as telling the truth: *I didn't make the deadline. I ordered the wrong product. I double-booked, so I missed the meeting. I screwed up.*

In that moment, you'll have to deal with the temporary negative ramifications, but what you've ultimately gained—even if it's down the road—is integrity and respect. The distinction of being *truthful*.

That may not make you popular, but it *does* make you interesting. Authenticity is much the same. You will find people will start looking at you like a beacon to guide them. Because everyone is walking around with their own layers, wearing them like armor, your very presence will be an inspiration. There's a simple peace that comes with knowing yourself, and I believe people are drawn to that.

If we are to build strong networks, then we have to do it from this place of authenticity—trusting in the uniqueness of who we have been created to be instead of burying it so deep that we have no chance of standing out.

Because what if we do want to stand out? Is that so bad? Recently, I was having a conversation with a friend on this topic, and I looked up the definition of that phrase: "stand out." I expected to find meanings that essentially alluded to someone who's attention-seeking or self-absorbed. What I found instead was this: "to be easily noticeable." And you know what? Another word for "noticeable" is *unmistakable*.

That struck me, and I started thinking about how easily we can become mistakable. How quickly we can be swept up in a current heading in a direction that's opposite of who we are and what we're truly about.

I read this anecdote from John MacArthur recently, and I couldn't shake the parallel it makes about our own authenticity. Supposedly, when in training to recognize counterfeits, federal treasury agents never study the bogus bills. They handle only the real money. The point is if you spend enough time with the genuine, you can easily spot a counterfeit.[1]

I'm not willing to backslide into operating under a counterfeit version of myself. It's not worth risking everything around me—from my marriage to my family to our company. And these things are just too valuable to consider compromising simply because I opted to pretend to be someone I'm not. That would be a betrayal to myself—and to anyone in my network who might be relying on me.

The reality is, authenticity is going to look completely different for you than it does for me. It may be that you feel sharpest in a bespoke three-piece suit or that you love talking about art history. All I'm saying is, physically or otherwise, don't get swept up in the current of fitting in. A network built on imitation won't have the strength to withstand all the pressures and complications life will throw at you.

But hear this: being authentic should not be confused with being immovable. Authenticity doesn't mean resisting change. It's not a stubborn resolve to stay the same forever—*this is me, take it or leave it.* It should be more fluid than that. I'm not telling you to carve out absolutes as much as I'm encouraging you to commit to checking in with yourself, to having that dialogue. To be in constant pursuit of identifying your nonnegotiables.

If you do that and you feel like your internal compass is spinning, go find yourself some quiet. Step back from the noise, the cell phone, the constant barrage of content. (Because it won't stop coming in until you choose to turn it off.)

**If you don't do the "you" part right, it's a whole lot
harder to do the "we" part right. #makesense**

Then consider who you spend your time with. Who do you go to for advice? Your network is only as authentic as the people within it. And that starts with you. If you're inauthentic, then, at best, the network you build will be inauthentic too. At worst, it can lead you to doubt who you really are.

We need to surround ourselves with people who are genuine. I'd rather have one true, authentic person on speed dial than a thousand yes-people. There are few more dangerous places for a leader to exist than an echo chamber. That's not what I want from the people in my network. I want to be called out, even when it stings. I want to be challenged, even when it's painful. It takes courage and empathy to disagree respectfully, but a willingness to speak truth, even if wounding, can be a telltale sign of authenticity.

As we start out on this journey toward a life of meaning, I want to encourage you with this: from your family to your relationships to your work, authenticity is an absolute necessity. It's nonnegotiable. If you don't value the qualities and traits you bring to the table, you'll be hard-pressed to find the courage and confidence to trust or lead those around you. If you don't do the "you" part right, it's a whole lot harder to do the "we" part right.

As long as we allow ourselves to be remade based on what other people think, then what we're really doing is handing them the pen and letting them determine who our character is and how our story will unfold. If we do that, there's a good chance we might never get that pen back. And that's a shame, because you get one life. One story to tell.

It's a vulnerable thing to show up fully as we are. And it's uncomfortable to share our *realness*, the parts of us that may bring vulnerability or shame to the surface. But I'll take a few moments of painful exposure over a lifetime of hiding in halfness. That's not living; that's just pretending.

People who are willing to negotiate everything don't stand for anything. By living to please everyone else, they lose sight of who they are. People who make authenticity nonnegotiable, on the other hand, erase the space between who they are and who they want to be. They aren't afraid to take a different path, even if it means blazing it themselves.

BOTTOM LINE

Living true to yourself is a Nonnegotiable.

CHAPTER 4

EXTRA-ORDINARY

My parents always knew I was cut from a different cloth. Mom used to tell people I was going to be a preacher when I grew up. Dad would add, "If he doesn't end up in jail first." Obviously, they didn't have a clue what I'd grow up to be, but they did their best to steer me toward what they thought was the right path. *Work hard and do well in school—that's the way to achieve success.*

My parents believed in the system that was in place to deliver a good life to someone willing to work for it. And boy, did I *work*. From the earliest days of my childhood, I'd been taught the value of hard work. Ours was a real blue-collar family. We never stopped. We'd work hard all week, and then on the weekends we would mow the grass. As a break we would pull weeds. You've never had more fun than the Gaines family doing lots and lots of basic, mundane chores, over and over again, in the middle of June, July, and August.

Dad brought that same belief in sweat equity to my baseball career.

Basically, from the time I could walk, my father and I set out to make me a great ball player. I was athletic enough and had natural skill, but I was no prodigy. So my dad used to tell me, "Gaineses have to work twice as hard."

There was not a single day that Dad let me forget this. When he picked me up from practice, he'd say, "How many laps did Coach have you guys run today?"

I'd tell him, "Twenty."

"Well, what if we went and did five more?" he'd say.

So we'd both get out of the car and head back to the field and bang out another five.

I trusted that Dad was right that what was required was just the starting line. That working harder was what it took to have a chance at success. And not just with athletics but with my future too.

I believed in working hard, but like I said in the last chapter, I didn't want to work hard just to end up where most people seemed to—in a steady job even if that job bored them to death. I didn't want to work hard for boring or for normal. I wanted to work hard for a shot at something extraordinary. I suspected I wasn't the only one who felt that way.

I had this feeling that there were people out there who, like me, felt most alive when they wandered a little outside the norm. Who lived life on their own terms, who weren't interested in doing things the ordinary way. Each time I'd meet or read about someone who would give me hope that there was a potential for something extraordinary, I'd clench my teeth and believe I just might be right—that there *was* another way. I just had to keep my eyes open for people who could show me how to find it.

You know the guys who take their metal detectors out to the park or to the beach? They sweep their wand, searching and searching, and mostly, they come up empty. They find more of what you'd expect—a few nails or maybe some bottle caps. But then one day, that thing starts beeping like crazy because they've found what they've been searching for.

That was me. I was out there with my sensor scanning for examples of people who had done things differently, whose lives were anything but ordinary. I was looking for people who had the first quality that is crucial to building a strong network: a drive to be extraordinary.

The folks I ended up finding might not have registered on everyone's radar. These weren't the gold nuggets glistening in the sunlight; they were more like diamonds in the rough. To see what made them valuable, you had to look below the surface.

One of my first finds was a guy named—are you ready for this?— Chip. Chip Smith was the dad of a girl I went to high school with. In suburban Dallas-Fort Worth, most parents had good jobs with notable companies like IBM and GE. They wore polished shoes and suits to their offices, where every day they sat behind their desks. That wasn't Chip Smith. He didn't work in an office, and he certainly didn't wear a suit. He was a pool builder. You could probably count on one hand the number of people who'd list that as their dream job.

What got me about him, though, was that the guy loved his work, and it showed. Where a lot of parents I knew looked like they'd spent their days working for companies whose purpose was to squeeze the life out of them, Chip looked like he'd spent the day on purpose. Whenever I saw him, he was smiling, with a flush in his cheeks and energy in his step. He looked, dressed, and acted differently. For sure, there were other parents who might have appeared more polished and sophisticated, but when Chip came into a room, you noticed. He always seemed to be having a heck of a lot more fun working in the cement than any of the other parents who came home carrying briefcases. It looked to seventeen-year-old me like he was living the dream his way. I wanted some of that—the confidence, the freedom, the fun—in whatever future I was going to carve out for myself.

But it wasn't often that I'd come across people like Chip, who looked like they were living out something unique. These sightings were so rare, so few and far between, that I'd start to think maybe the well-worn road was the only road after all.

I think this happens to a lot of us. If you think back to your childhood, those days in middle school, you can probably recall some desire that was totally unique and maybe a little unorthodox. Our culture teaches us that conformity is your highest probability of success. Or, at the very least, the path of least resistance. So then you thought, *I should just do it the way Mom and Dad told me to,* or *I'm going to do what my coach said.*. and so on. Or you were told not to ask too many questions. Maybe you didn't want to rock the boat or make things more complicated. And without realizing it, you gave in.

Even if we start out living as ourselves, as we get older, the message of conformity around us grows louder and louder. *Hedge your bets. Stay in your lane.* And we start to believe that message.

Without a clear path to take, I did what I'd always been told I would have to do in order to succeed. After a year at a local junior college, I applied to Baylor University and got in. I thought my mom's heart would burst when I got that acceptance letter. Hey, I was excited too. Surely I'd find people there who lived a life guided by passion and enthusiasm instead of by the book. Turned out I was right, but not in the way I expected.

UNDERESTIMATE AT YOUR OWN RISK

When I got to Baylor, it became abundantly clear that I wasn't going to magically transform into a star student just because I was at an institution of higher learning. My grades, my attention, my interest—all of it was lacking. I struggled to engage. Maybe I could have, if I'd felt even remotely confident that college was a means to an end actually suited for me. Yet with each passing semester, it was feeling more and more like boot camp for a mission I didn't believe in. I might have given up hope if it wasn't for Uncle Ricky.

Ricky is the uncle of a college friend. Where Chip Smith possessed a sort of suave confidence, what I saw in Uncle Ricky was an insatiable desire to live a life worth writing about. To not just read about history but make himself a part of it.

Uncle Ricky lives in the East Texas town of Jacksonville. He came from the old country. His ancestors were cattlemen, and his father owned the local grocery store. Like mine, his school days had been marked by an eagerness to just get out and get to work. He and his wife, Cindy, own a gorgeous thirty-acre property with a barn, chapel, chicken house, carriage house, and the crown jewel—a carefully constructed Southern home. They built everything themselves, but to look at it, you'd think it was a couple hundred years old.

Uncle Ricky might give you a misleading impression at first glance. If you showed up at his farm and saw Ricky in his overalls and trucker hat, you might be surprised to learn that he's a successful lawyer. I know I was. But as he told me story after story about how he's won countless cases in court because his opponents had grossly underestimated his intellect, I took that don't-judge-a-book-by-its-cover lesson to heart.

When my buddies and I would go out to visit in the summer, we'd find Ricky in his overalls, riding his tractor or tending to his animals early in the morning before he went into the office. He was the kind of guy who kept on working after a full day's work. He'd go out to the barn and build or tinker with a side project until midnight and be mad when he'd have to stop for sleep. He had passion like I'd never seen. His endless capacity to apply himself totally resonated with me. That was the thing about him: he refused to dedicate his life to just one thing. Where everyone else would say that someone with his legal smarts should put everything into that practice, he let his interests range far and wide. I was drawn to that.

Uncle Ricky was the first person I met who turned the concept of balance on its head. His life, like his great estate in Texas, had room for all of it—work, family, and hobbies. There was truly no limit to his activities and interests.

Ricky still travels the world, collecting priceless antiques and repurposing them on his farm. Even today, every time I show up, Ricky has something new to show me—a Civil War–era rolltop desk or paneling from a French cathedral that was bombed in World War II. He never ceases to pick up a new interest or grand pursuit. He's a constant reminder of how full life can be if you refuse to put limits on yourself.

I planted Ricky on my mental map to my future, one more coordinate I could use to show me the way. Obviously law school wasn't even remotely a prospect for me. But it wasn't his profession that I was drawn to. It was his passion for life.

By my senior year of college, getting my diploma was basically just for sport. I knew I wasn't going to rely on it the way other kids might. I had spent more time starting businesses and mowing lawns than I had studying for exams. I still wasn't entirely sure where I was headed after graduation. In my final stretch of schooling, I almost—*almost*—turned to walk on the well-trodden path.

Just as I had one foot out the door of Baylor, I stepped into the only class I was ever any good at. On the first day, I took my seat in the back, but I quickly realized that I was the only student in a course called "Professional Selling" who had any sales experience. The professor, Dr. Tanner, took a shine to me. Several weeks into class, after I'd shown some promise, he pulled me aside.

"Chip," he said, "there's an opportunity that's come up, and I think it's perfect for you. It's a position as a copier salesman at an international copier company. It would be a good first job and a great starting salary."

"Wow," I said. "I'll definitely think about it."

He was probably hoping for a little more enthusiasm. Especially from a kid with my below-average grades who really should have been thankful for *any* job lead, much less an incredible opportunity like this one was.

I'd be lying if I didn't say that at some level I *was* interested. Who wouldn't be? It was the kind of corporate position my classmates would've killed for. For them, it would've justified all those hours in the library, all that tuition spent. And for me, a guy about to graduate with a two-point-nothing GPA, it should have looked like a life raft. A set future.

When I told my parents about the opportunity, they made it clear that I'd be an idiot not to grab that raft and hold on to it for dear life. They even went out and bought me my first sport coat for the interview. My friends agreed. Here was my chance to begin life as a grown-up.

"This is a huge job," my buddies said. "And you'd be making *real* money."

As a senior in college, I was already bringing in about thirty grand a year from my lawn business, which was nothing to scoff at, but I was completely killing myself for it. While my friends were bowling or going out for Mexican food, I'd be buzzing around on a lawnmower, trying to finish before I lost the last of daylight. What moron would continue that backbreaking effort with no guarantee? What Dr. Tanner was offering me was a near foolproof chance to succeed.

All I had to do was ignore that every cell in my body was screaming, *Don't do it!*

The universe is hilarious. The job being dangled in front of me, tempting me to be just like everyone else, was selling *copiers*, machines that churn out identical copies one after another. I got the hint.

Dr. Tanner was right; I was a born salesman. But if I were to take the job, I knew how that story would go. Learn the ropes, get promoted,

and repeat until retirement. I thought about the dozens of successful men and women I knew who had done exactly that after college. Then I thought about Chip and Uncle Ricky.

Like them, I always felt like there was something off when I looked around and saw everyone doing the same thing, as if they were carbon copies. I'd wonder, *Are you guys not seeing what I'm seeing?*

I went back to Dr. Tanner's class a few days later and let him know that I had turned down the job. My poor parents. When they sent me off to Baylor, it might as well have been Yale. They'd done just about everything they could to ensure my future would be brighter than theirs. And there I was, turning down a sensible job, a choice that left me right back where I started—mowing lawns.

For me, though, sticking with my gut was worth the risk of giving up the guaranteed career. I knew I was headed for a different path, one I'd need to grab a machete, head into the woods, and forge for myself.

When I was in my twenties, I discovered the book *Rich Dad Poor Dad* by Robert Kiyosaki. The book presents a parable about a boy who learns financial lessons from watching two different types of dads. The boy's father, Poor Dad, encourages his son to work hard and seek security. But his friend's father, Rich Dad, encourages him to pursue wealth through entrepreneurship and smart investments. Basically, pitting the traditional path against a self-guided tour. Poor Dad touts stability and punching a clock to get the one check stub every two weeks. Rich Dad champions experience—the hard knocks that come from teaching yourself—and multiple streams of income. Poor Dad wants his son to climb the ladder, while the Rich Dad wants him to own the ladder.

It rocked my world to read *in a book* that putting your head down and working hard only to follow the herd wasn't the only path to success. I was starting to realize that success, for me, wasn't going to be a question of working hard. It was more about what I'd be working *toward*.

I'm grateful every single day for the work ethic my father instilled in me. I still work twice as hard, and I genuinely enjoy putting in a hard day's work. But *Rich Dad Poor Dad* opened my eyes to a new prospect. Maybe working hard could also mean working different. Maybe it could mean taking risks and expanding my expectations. My dad had busted his butt giving me the ability to develop my talents. Maybe one of those talents could be finding my own way.

That's what I want for you. Whatever path you're on, how could you look differently at opportunities along the way? Maybe wander a little from where you thought you were headed. You might be surprised where you end up.

I don't want to overstate it, but at the time I didn't know many other people on the planet who thought about things this way. With the rare exception of a handful of guys like Chip and Ricky, I'd been surrounded by influences my whole life who, with the best intentions, had told me to play it safe. But after I read that book, I felt validated. I knew if I had to choose between climbing the ladder and owning it, I'd choose none of the above. I'd just build my own ladder.

The thing about building your own ladder is that even though you get to decide where to put it and how high to extend it, there isn't necessarily anyone at the bottom holding it steady for you. The way my career unfolded, there have been plenty of moments when I thought for sure I was going to come tumbling down.

You probably know the basics of Jo's and my careers—lawn care, renovation, Magnolia, *Fixer Upper*—but you might not know how many times we came within pennies of Googling "how to file for bankruptcy."

Jo and I have always been learners at our cores, so once we were married and in business together we decided that if we were going to do this thing, we were really going to do it. Early on we knew that rather than conforming to how things have always been done, we were going to go head-first into the challenge of forging our own path. As I've said, I'm not one for business plans. I don't want to pour hours into creating a document with charts and graphs and a whole financial summary and market analysis of a business that doesn't even exist yet, and then hand that document over to a couple of bankers who, in most cases, never owned a business in their lives. In fairness, they've seen thousands of business plans. They are experts in business plans. But I'm not looking to write a killer business plan. I'm looking to create a killer business. For my money, I'd rather go ahead and do the thing and figure it out as I go.

As Magnolia started to grow, we didn't concern ourselves too much with what others were doing in the marketplace. Not because we thought we knew better than everyone else, but because we believed our hearts were leading us toward something different than the way things have always been done.

Let me tell you, things went wrong at least as often as they went right. Because of the choices we'd made, we were constantly building proverbial castles in the sand. When we started our renovation business, we'd fix up something uninhabitable, sell it for a little profit, and then have to start over again.

While my college buddies were driving around in Range Rovers—their car notes alone were more than my mortgage—our finances were constantly up and down. I brought our first baby home to an eight-hundred-square-foot house. It seemed everyone around me—those who had taken the corporate-type gigs—was making money hand over fist. But here I was, the one everyone had voted "Most Likely to Succeed," and all the money we had was tied up in projects. A less stubborn man might have seen that all the signs seemed to be saying it was time to stop dreaming the irrational dream and just find a "real" job. A paycheck every two weeks starts to look pretty good when you're constantly in the red.

When I say we were in the red, I don't mean that like "Oh, we could only afford to go out to dinner once a week." I mean we owed people thousands of dollars. What we were doing wasn't exactly robbing Peter to pay Paul, but we were definitely borrowing from Peter to pay Paul and then hoping like crazy that Peter didn't come to collect too soon. I'm joking, of course, but it was almost that bad. Then we'd go a few months thinking we just might make it. It was always feast or famine.

For years it went on like this. I'd rolled the dice with our lives. No doubt there were seasons that were very scary—but never as scary as the idea of not living life on our own terms.

The more people told me I needed to reverse course and be a little more conventional, the harder I worked to prove there was a different way to succeed.

That's what I'd loved most about Uncle Ricky and Chip. They were their own most trusted guides. The best Sherpa in the world can't take you somewhere he's never been. You've got to draw your own map. The only person who can help you figure out how to live life according to your own terms is you.

**Whatever you're doing, make sure it lights a fire in you *and* that
you were the one who struck the match. #makesense**

We get only one chance at this life, and I am not willing to follow someone else's map. That's the surest way I know to veer off the path I'm meant to find for myself. Pretty soon, I'd get lost inside someone else's idea of how to live. It happens so often that it's not even remarkable. It's the norm. I once saw a quote from Kierkegaard that read, "The greatest hazard of all, losing one's self, can occur very quietly in the world, as if it were nothing at all. No other loss can occur so quietly; any other loss—an arm, a leg, five dollars, a wife, etc.—is sure to be noticed."[1] That blew me away. Why are we so willing to let other people's ideas of what success looks like keep us from living as ourselves?

I want to add a qualifier here. Living outside the system is what has worked for me. Your definition of what's extraordinary might look totally different. In fact, I hope it does! Maybe safety and security are your passion. Maybe you swoon at the idea of waking up well rested because you know that you have enough savings in the bank to take care of yourself if something should happen. Keep the steady job if it means more time with family. Choose the nine-to-five so you can spend evenings working on something you're passionate about. If it means that you'll get to love your family better or catch more ball games, by all means, don't waste a second doing anything else.

Whatever you're doing, make sure it lights a fire in you *and* that you were the one who struck the match. Wherever you find your passion—at work, at home, or both—when you do, time becomes your jet fuel. I think about how mad Uncle Ricky was at the sun for setting every day. He wanted to be out there doing what he loved as long as he could.

We don't seek the extraordinary merely to serve ourselves. I'm not telling you to do your own thing purely so that you can feel some level of satisfaction about your life. That's just a bonus. Think about your legacy.

Your *living* legacy—at this very moment you are writing it. If you're not fulfilling your highest aspirations, then I want to challenge you. Don't concede to the safe path just because some other yahoo told you it's what you're supposed to do. The Siren of security sings a pretty sweet song, but if you want to live an extraordinary life, there is nothing like the beat of your own drum.

BOTTOM LINE

Never underestimate the EXTRA-ordinary.

CHAPTER 5

SWERVE

Consider this: You hop in the car to go somewhere you've gone a million times before—the office, your sister's house, your kid's school. You start the engine, turn on the radio, and make the first turn out of the driveway. Next thing you know, you're at your destination with no earthly idea of how you got there. I mean, you know in your head you must have stopped at the light at the end of your street and gotten on the freeway, but the part of your brain that should have recorded those memories is just blank. It's almost like you went into a time warp. That drive is gone to you. But if at some point during that drive something unexpected happens—someone cuts you off or an animal darts across the road—it can snap you out of your dream state and make you swerve into another lane. Suddenly, you're hyperalert. Time slows down. Every frame is seared into your memory— the cracks in the highway, the feeling of sweat between your hands and the steering wheel, the way your body sways with the car, the screech of your tires. Something about that swerve wakes you right up.

Without even knowing it, a lot of us have set our lives to cruise control, doing things today because that's how we did them yesterday. But I'll bet some of you have experienced a moment where *something* or *someone* lands in your path by surprise, waking you up and shocking you into a new way of thinking, a new way of living. You don't always see it coming, but it'll make you grab the wheel for dear life—and, if you're ready, cause you to change direction.

I experienced my first big swerve when I was in college.

Now, I know you didn't come to this book looking for a Chip Gaines baseball memoir, but bear with me a second because, as you'll see, this story isn't really about baseball.

You probably know by now that for my first twenty or so years a bat and glove defined my life. You probably also know that I've always been a bit of a wisecracker, and I didn't take a time out from cracking wise just because I was on the baseball field. I was always messing around, shooting my mouth off, or pranking my teammates. My junior college coach must have threatened to kick me off the team five or ten times for saying something smart-alecky or doing some stupid thing. But every time I saw him getting a little hot under the collar, I relied on my charm to get back into his good graces. And it usually worked. In fact, my charm usually worked on everyone.

But then I met Coach Smith.

When Coach Smith took over the Baylor baseball program my sophomore year, it was immediately clear that the man did not mess around. He was a sniper-level straight shooter, and when I say he didn't mess around, I mean the man Did. Not. Mess. Around.

One afternoon, after we'd been practicing with him a few weeks, he called a meeting and told the team, "Boys, I've never seen worse baserunning. Some clown got picked off three times. We didn't even have the steal signal on any of those three times. What is going on?"

I'd give you three guesses who that clown was, but you probably wouldn't need the other two. I burned a little inside knowing that I'd screwed up during practice, but no biggie, I could always smooth things over.

Coach wrapped up the meeting, and I walked up to him while the locker-room bustle was settling down. I put my arm around this guy I barely knew and said, "Listen, Coach, I just want you to know, whichever clown got picked off three times, I'll do whatever it takes to get that guy whipped into shape. I'll stay late with him. I'll run laps with him. You tell me what he needs, and I'll make sure he gets it."

I pulled back a little and looked at Coach Smith's face, expecting him to crack a smile and say something like, "Well, you know, you got on base three times. That's not too bad, son. We can work on the base-running part." But there was no smile. Instead, he just lifted my arm off his shoulder and brushed it off without a word.

I figured out pretty quickly that Coach Smith was a go-getter and he was aiming to remake the program. Before long, he started making cuts to the team. I was relieved to make it through the first round, but then, a few days later, Coach called me in, along with a couple of other players. He was gracious about it, which I always appreciated. He could have just stuck a list of names on his door with a thumbtack, but he had the decency to meet with us in person. He made it clear that he thought we were capable and qualified, but what he had in mind for the future didn't include us.

I left the building that day hoping it was all just a bad dream. Maybe I'd wake up tomorrow and this wouldn't have happened. But nope. It was real. The very next day, we turned in our gear. It might as well have been my kidneys I was handing over to the equipment manager. It felt like a funeral. There were a few kids who had been happy just to be on the team in the first place, so they were bummed, but they rallied and turned their attention to their classes or their girlfriends or their fraternities or some other element of the college experience. But for me, baseball *was* the college experience.

I'm not sure if I was depressed or what, but I'd say I was definitely in denial. I kept parking my pickup at the baseball fields like I always had and walking to class from there, like I couldn't get it through my head that I wasn't on the team anymore. Talk about being on autopilot. I'd defined myself in relation to the game for so long, I wasn't sure I knew who I was without it.

It was right around that time that I met a guy named Brian. And he woke me the heck up.

Brian wasn't a ballplayer, but he hung out with enough of the guys on the team that he was in our larger circle. I hadn't known him well my first year, but I'd seen him around and I knew who he was. He was hard to miss on account of his glass eye, which he'd gotten in high school.

The way Brian tells it, he and his buddies were goofing off in the woods one day with a few makeshift blow darts they'd built using cardboard from old coat hangers and sewing needles. You can probably guess how Brian lost his right eye without much more information than that. Can you imagine what that was like in high school? I mean a single zit or the wrong T-shirt can get you ruthlessly made fun of, and this guy strolls into school with *a glass eye*. If that bothered him, he didn't show it; he always had this internal confidence and an overall likability about him.

One day, while I was still in a funk about baseball, Brian and I were hanging around with a bunch of guys on campus and we got to talking. He made an offhand reference to something that had happened when he'd been working out a few months earlier. I had no idea what he was talking about. Seems he had been lifting weights in the rec center one day and had been hit with an intense headache, like a lightning bolt to the skull. Before he knew what was what, he blacked out. A few seconds later, he came to. He shook it off and tried to go back to life as usual, but before long he had a few more episodes. After some tests, his doctors found an aneurysm and told Brian he'd have to have brain surgery. It was at this point he pulled back his hair to show me the question-mark-shaped scar etched into his forehead.

"Man," he said, "I can't believe you didn't hear about this." Neither could I. I'd been so caught up in my navel-gazing that not even someone in my circle having a near-death experience had gotten through to me. This guy had already lost his eye in a freak blow-dart accident, then he nearly died. No one would have blamed the dude if he skulked around campus trailing a cloud of bitterness and anger around him like Pigpen. But he wasn't mucking around in self-pity. He was out there living, radiating positivity.. and here I was getting down because I was cut from the baseball team? It woke me up. Brian showed me I could either keep driving to the practice field each day on autopilot, fantasizing about getting back on the team, or I could choose to see the life in front of me.

A DAILY DOZEN

Of the thousands of decisions we face each day, we make the majority on autopilot, but it doesn't have to be that way. You have the power to click off cruise control. For the next week, challenge yourself to make twelve decisions you usually wouldn't make. Does that sound like a lot? Well, that's the point. I want you on your toes, active, engaged, and deliberate, instead of sleepwalking through life. Start small. Drink tea instead of coffee, turn left instead of right, dress up or dress down, go in the back door, start a meeting by celebrating your team, play hooky, read a different newspaper, skip your workout for a day if it's become mundane. Or hit the gym if it's been a while. If you want a different result, you've got to take a different action. Get in the habit of breaking habits.

There seem to be two types of people in the world: people who pay attention to where they are headed, ready to shift gears whenever necessary, and people who are living another life in their heads while the world keeps on spinning. I think folks in this second group are more likely to wake up one day to find themselves living in the most depressing town you can imagine. For the sake of this example, let's call it Regret City.

In Regret City, one day is the same as the next. You spend your days mooning over what you *aren't* doing and what you could have done instead if the cards had fallen differently. Nothing ever changes, including you. Once you get there, it's awfully hard to leave—like there's a force field keeping you inside. Citizens of Regret City while away their precious days, not awake and engaged but dreaming of what might have been.

Look, you can spend an awful lot of your life lamenting that you are not living a different one. But you know what's happening while you're fantasizing about another life? You're wasting the one you've got. You only get so much time, so many heartbeats. How are you going to use it—fantasizing about what life might be like in some alternate universe or discovering the beauty of the one you live in now?

After meeting Brian, I started daydreaming about what my future could look like, a future that didn't include baseball. It was like Plato's "Allegory of the Cave"—the parable he tells about what it's like to have your eyes opened. The story goes that there are prisoners who have been chained since birth in a dank underground cave, forced to watch shadows cast on the wall in front of them. That's all they've seen their whole life, so as far as they know, that's what life is: flat shadows on the slimy wall of the cave. They've never seen a goat, so for all they know, the shadow of a goat *is* a goat.

When one prisoner is released and brought outside, the bright light stings his eyes and disorients him. Once he is told that the things he is seeing are real, at first he has trouble getting his head around it, but his eyes gradually adjust and he finally manages to see things as they are.[1] You can imagine what happens when he comes back into the dark to tell his friends what he's seen. They think he's nuts.

My point here is when someone comes into your life to show you you've been staring at a bunch of shadow puppets, you can either dismiss them and go back to staring at that wall or you can slide out of your shackles and walk toward the light.

That's how it was for me. Once I'd seen the light come streaming in, I couldn't go back to the way things had been. My eyes were open, and I went from looking backward at baseball to looking forward to what might be, what *could be*, next. If I'd still been moping around in the dark, I might not have noticed the Montblanc pen of my classmate who introduced me to sales. Or heard the hum of the lawnmower outside my classroom, which ultimately led me to start my first real business. I sure wouldn't have gained the lens to see the potential in the houses that became the first Magnolia homes.

Looking back, I wonder if I would have liked being a ballplayer even if I had beaten the odds and continued my career. Yes, I would have been playing a sport I loved dearly, but I sure as heck would not have the family or career I have now. If I had decided to double down on base-ball, I would have been forcing something that was not meant to be *and* missing out on all that was.

You know what's happening while you're fantasizing about another life? You're wasting the one you've got. #makesense

I'm grateful I swerved in time. I have Brian to thank in part for that. No one could have scripted what happened to Brian next. His junior year, Brian was diagnosed with testicular cancer. By the time he found out, it had already spread to his lymph nodes, liver, and lungs. Cancer doesn't fight fair, but Brian handled it the same way he handled his glass eye and brain surgery—with wit and grace and positivity. Not once did I witness him moaning about his lot in life, wishing he were someone else.

What about you? Are you living life in the here and now or is your vision stuck staring at the shadows? Is there someone in your circle who reminds you to stay focused on what's ahead instead of replaying the past or wondering what might have been? If so, hold on to them.

At some level, I think I've always been aware of how precious time is. I have two recurring dreams that I can't help but interpret as reminders that time is fleeting. In the first one, I'm negotiating with a bank teller to give me $5,000 so I can go back and bargain with someone else who's in a position to grant me another thirty-eight minutes of life. In the other dream, I'm leaving a voice message on someone's answering machine, the old-fashioned kind that used to cut you off after two minutes, and I'm going on and on about who knows what, and then I hear *beeeeep* before I've had a chance to say my piece.

Just in case I wasn't getting the message clear enough, a few years ago I got another reminder. If you've followed my story, chances are you've heard about my friend Gabe and how my life changed when I met her back in 2017.

I was in New York City doing promotion for the publication of my book *Capital Gaines*. I was in Central Park between interviews, and I was jacking around trying to get a bunch of busy New Yorkers to pay attention to a five-dollar bill I'd tied to a string (don't ask). Truth be told, I was a little sulky.

As much as I appreciate that folks are interested in the work that Jo

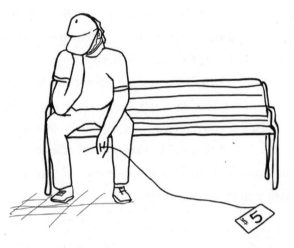

and I are doing, sometimes going on those shows feels like playing the part of Chip Gaines rather than actually *being* Chip Gaines. That was right around the time that Jo and I had decided to leave *Fixer Upper*—for similar reasons. When it started, authenticity was the life breath of the show. Jo and I doing our thing was what producers called "a breath of fresh air." We were so grateful to have found this strange place where we could be ourselves, and it spoke to people. But as time progressed and things got more formulaic, I felt boxed in. In TV, there's a phrase they use—"structured reality." It's kind of like saying "based on a true story." And I had gotten to the point where I was losing the truth of my story.

It started to wear on me that people were referring to my house and our construction sites as "on set." Those weren't sets; that was my *home* and our *work*. It was my life. Not just a background for a good TV show. I didn't want props and lights. I wanted proof of life. I needed things to be authentic again. I don't think I'd fully processed my feelings about leaving the show at that point, so I was glad to be able to focus on the book for a while.

Anyway, as I was sitting there, this guy ran past me a few times, and I decided to holler at him, asking how long it would take a lump like me to train for a marathon. He held up four fingers to indicate four months, but he didn't miss a step. He passed me a couple more times, but he wasn't about to interrupt his run for some yahoo who looked completely incapable of running a mile, let alone a marathon.

Just as I was about to go back to my five-dollar-bill game, he came by for a final lap. This time, he was with a woman, who, as luck would have it, recognized me. She persuaded him to take a break and shoot the breeze with me for a few minutes. As we talked, I learned his name was Justin and her name was Gabriele, and that she was a professional run-ner.. I'm talking *world-class athlete*. I can only imagine how much hard work and determination that takes.

I was interested in that, of course, but I also couldn't help but be curious about the massive thirteen-inch scar running down Gabe's torso. Turns out, that scar was from a surgery she'd had to remove half of her liver. She explained that she had adenoid cystic carcinoma (ACC), a rare salivary cancer that had spread through her body. She'd started a foundation to support rare-cancer research to empower cancer survivors through physical activity. Are you ready for this? After the surgery that gave her the scar, she had been back up and running only three months later. Three months! *Holy cow*, I thought, *here's a woman who didn't let something as serious as cancer slow her down, and here I am feeling stuck in neutral, not sure where our lives are headed after* Fixer Upper.

That moment I realized I could walk away with nothing more than the memory of a nice conversation with an impressive stranger, or I could grab the baton Gabe held out for me and try to run toward something that might make a difference. It was a moment of clarity. There was *no way* I was going to look back a year later and think, *Oh yeah, remember that gal with the wicked scar in Central Park who was such a beast of determination and passion? I wish I had listened more closely to that feeling that came from a chance encounter.*

I made the decision right then and there. I was going to run a mara-thon, Magnolia was going to host it, and the proceeds would benefit the

NO PAIN, NO GAINES

Brave Like Gabe Foundation. And about four months later, we hosted the first Silo District Marathon.

Gabe graciously agreed to help me figure out a training schedule. It had been ages since I had run so much as a footrace with my kids, and I'm not going to lie: it was tough. I'd forgotten how far a mile was—let alone twenty-six of them. As much as my fortysomething-year-old dad bod wanted to, Gabe would not let me quit. There were times when it was tempting, but then I'd think about Gabe and her scar and smile to match and think, *Are you kidding me? It's time to lace up.*

As I got to know Gabe, what inspired me most about her was her refusal to let cancer define her. She didn't just want to get better and be cancer free; she wanted to be *fast*, to keep running. She didn't want to be known only as a person with cancer. The "About" page of her website has the tagline "Pro runner. Rare cancer advocate. Relentless optimist." That about says it all. Cancer didn't come first. Running came first, then advocating, and then optimism anchored her. She was a world-class athlete, and when cancer ensnared her, she knew she had a choice—she could be a victim, or she could keep pursuing the thing she loved best in life. Running was her passion, and she wasn't willing to live her life in reverse.

Four months of training passed quickly, and race day was every-thing I'd hoped it would be. Gabe joined me at mile nineteen, at which point I'd started walking. As soon as she ran up, she looked me dead in the face and said, "It's going to hurt whether you walk or whether you run—so I say let's run and just get it over with!" That kick in the pants from Gabe was what helped me push through. I crossed the finish line with my daughter Emmie Kay by my side. That day, together with all the other runners, we were able to raise $250,000 for the Brave Like Gabe Foundation.

Two Silo District Marathons later, Gabe was still running profession-ally while battling cancer. Then, one afternoon Jo and I got a call from

Justin. Gabe had taken a sudden turn. Her fight, it seemed, was nearing an end. We'd known the odds, but the news hit me like a sledgehammer to the heart. This girl who had bounded down the streets of Waco smiling and waving with me was now struggling through her final days.

Gabe was no ordinary woman. She was as kind and gracious as she was strong and resilient. She showed me there is glory in the resolve to never give up. And then she showed me there can be equal glory in the grace to surrender. To know when you have run the race well and have fought the good fight. Gabe lived both beautifully.

It has been my experience that when you encounter someone in person, when you actually breathe the same air as them, see the wrinkles they've earned and scars they carry, you understand their story in a deep way. And if you're paying attention, if you're open to letting them shape you, that's when you swerve. You wake up and use that adrenaline rush as jet fuel to thrust you forward.

Chances are it won't be someone you've known since you were in braces. Someone you spend twenty minutes with might have more of an impact on you than a person you've known your whole life.

When you meet a person like Gabe or Brian, you can smile and watch from the sidelines, or you can let their dedication to living without regret and toward purpose pull you into a life of meaning. You can take that jolt and do something with it. Figure out what inspired you. What did it make you want to do or change about how you've been living? What can you learn from how they approach life that you can incorporate into your own? Then decide what you are going to do tomorrow. Go tell ten people. Then ten more people. Tell your wife or your husband. And then get up and actually *do the dang thing*.

I wish I could be the one to crash into your life and light a fire under you, but if we never meet, I hope I can help you understand the value of catching flame when someone like Brian or Gabe blazes into your life close enough to feel their heat.

In my life, I've found God to be ironic, symbolic, and divinely intentional with dates. I met Gabe on the day of my first book release, a book in which I'd joked about running marathons without having trained a single step. Two years later, in the very hours before Gabe's death, we were able to raise over $2 million for St. Jude and the Brave Like Gabe Foundation. And it all came from a chance encounter in the park.

From Brian and Gabe, I learned how to see each day as a gift, a check you're going to cash, a chance to lace up your shoes and hit the track. If you can somehow appreciate that, if you can see the sand slipping from the hourglass, then maybe you'll realize the minutes are too precious to be squandered. So get out there and keep running, and let Regret City fade away in your rearview mirror.

BOTTOM LINE

When life sends you someone who rips you out of your routine, pay attention!

CHAPTER 6

UNCOMFORTABLY KIND

It hit me like a sucker punch. When I picked up my phone that Sunday morning in August, I saw that the unthinkable had happened again—a mass shooting, the second in twenty-four hours.

My eyes scrolled over the screen. *Nine people killed outside a bar in Dayton, Ohio, including the gunman's own sister.* Blood and tears. More pain.

Only hours before, I'd gone to bed with images of the shooting in El Paso still in my head. Twenty-two people dead and dozens injured.

I sat down, taking it in. It seemed like every day there was something in the news that could break your heart. The thing was, as much as I hated to admit it, lots of times I felt numb to the reports. I'd read something awful about a terrible event that had happened halfway around the world—a natural disaster, a refugee crisis, a terror attack—and if you had asked me about it, I 100 percent would have shaken my head and said, "What a tragedy. I'll be praying for those people." And I would've meant it. But if I am cross-my-heart honest about it, after that little moment of recognition and some prayers, I would move on with my life. Get back to my own problems, my own world, my own people.

But these two shootings, back-to-back like that, I couldn't just brush them off and go back to what I was doing. I was shaken. Rattled. The fact that these two shootings happened nearly in tandem, and one of them in my home state, interrupted my ability to move on, to slide back into my comfortable life.

I was left with two questions: How did we get here? And how had I let myself get so numb?

Mother Teresa said, "If we have no peace, it is because we have forgotten that we belong to each other."[1] I take this to mean that we have stopped being kind to one another, stopped being compassionate. Frankly, I think we're pretty good at remembering that we belong to those who are closest to us, the people inside the bubble we enclose ourselves in. If your kid falls off her bike, you rush right over there to brush the dirt off. If your buddy gets sick, you bring his family a warm meal and offer to help in any way you can. But how far does that circle of compassion extend? To your neighbor? To a stranger? To someone who lives on the other side of the planet? It's like we've decided, *These people over here, my people? I see what they're about. I understand their hearts. But those people over there—I don't understand them at all. They're outside my bubble. They don't belong to me. Not my people. Not my problem.*

The thought was starting to settle over me that those shootings *were* my people, which makes it my problem.

What is keeping us from remembering that we belong to one another—*all* of us? The fact is we are literally made up of the same raw materials put together from the same atoms that have existed from the dawn of time. We have minds and hearts full of passions and hopes and flaws and jokes and quirks, things we'd like to shout from the mountain-tops, things we hope no one ever discovers about us, fears about being misunderstood, pain when something hurts. We are all deeply, funda-mentally, irrevocably human. How has it become so comfortable to treat each other as anything less?

The sad truth is things are easier when we let ourselves forget that we all belong to one another. If we don't have to worry about other peo-ple's feelings or lives, we can just go about our own.

When we're out of the comfort zone of our people, we tend to go into me-first mode. We take that parking spot even though someone else was clearly waiting for it. We use dismissive, disrespectful language on the internet. We pass up the fellow on the street experiencing homelessness who's holding a sign that says "please help" because we've stopped seeing him as a person. He's become as much a part of the landscape to us as the tree he is leaning on.

When someone is talking loudly next to you in a café and you move tables so you don't hear them anymore, you have removed yourself from the discomfort, but that doesn't mean they are speaking any quieter. Same deal with other people's pain. Just because you distance yourself from it doesn't mean their pain doesn't exist.

Putting on blinders to each other's humanity is how we end up with people calling each other savages, deplorables, animals, you name it. That's how we end up with the churches and synagogues with bullet holes, with knees on necks, with rage painting the internet, with accu-sations flying. That's how we end up in shouting matches with people whose ideas are even slightly different from our own. That's how we end up retreating to our own little silos of safety and sameness.

We have somehow fooled ourselves into thinking that we can't understand each other, and that is just one more obstacle that keeps us from showing each other kindness.

Over the past twenty years, we've worked with a lot of tough people in the construction business. People who have lived through some pretty gnarly circumstances. Most of these guys tend to keep their distance at first. They don't volunteer much about their lives or shoot the breeze during work, but I'm the guy who can't help but push a little bit.. then a little bit more. I'll keep nudging and being curious about their lives, including the hard parts. Sometimes, their thick skin is so thick that it would take weeks, but if I kept at it with real sincere interest, eventually they'd start answering me, and I'd learn about their financial hardships, health struggles, or whatever else was weighing them down. Each time that happened, their countenance shifted. It got a little lighter. They'd go from being grumpy and short to grudgingly grateful that someone took the time to ask after them. Sometimes, all it takes is a little push to encourage people to share their burdens. I really believe we aren't meant to carry them alone.

Those guys have always been a reminder to me that it's impossible to know what's going on below the surface of someone's life unless we take the time to ask, or at the very least, consider the full picture of where they are coming from.

Next time someone is short with you in line at the grocery store, instead of chalking it up to that person being a jerk, ask yourself if maybe there's something going on in that person's life that would make it hard for them to find the energy to be polite. What might that person have been doing five minutes before you ran into them? Really imagine it. Try thinking about what they might have been doing five hours earlier. Or five years. Do them the service of seeing them as a person with a history, a person who has a huge web of experiences that pulls on them every day, in the same way you do.

My point is to be as generous in your assumptions about people out-side your social circle as you are with those closest to you.

There's a scene in *Les Misérables* that makes this point crystal clear.

This thief, Jean Valjean, spent nineteen years in prison for stealing bread (because his family was starving). After his release, he found himself staying in the home of a bishop. The bishop served him a nice dinner with his finest silver, and the next morning, what did Jean Valjean do? He panicked. Because he'd been in freakin' prison. He didn't plan to, but he robbed the poor bishop blind. Hours later, when the French police dragged Hugh Jackman—I mean Jean Valjean—before the bishop and presented him as a thief, the bishop insisted the silver was a gift.

"Before you go away, here are your candlesticks; take them," the bishop said and put his last candlesticks in Jean Valjean's trembling hands. Here's the real kicker: the bishop then told him, "When you come again, you needn't come through the garden. You can always come and go by the front door."

The bishop wrapped up his spiel with a line that's the epitome of kindness and mercy: "Do not forget.. use this silver to become an honest man."[2]

Kindness begets kindness.

Making the choice to engage with dignity and respect for someone's human heart could mean the difference between living in a world that continues to throw stones and one that instead chooses to extend love and kindness.

As I continued to grapple with those shootings, I wondered—in each of those shooters' lives, what opportunities did we, collectively, have to treat them with kindness but chose not to? I'm not trying to pass the buck from those who did these terrible acts. The decisions they made are inexcusable. The actions they took are indefensible. I'm simply asking a question: *What if someone along the way had done something that reminded these guys that we belong to one another?* Might that shift in perspective have been the thing to derail them? The course of history could have been changed. That may sound naive to some, but you can't disregard that it's at least possible.

MAKE KINDNESS LOUD

The power of kindness was not a new thought to Jo and me. This concept is echoed in our Magnolia Manifesto, a series of statements that lead out the work we do as a company, serving as a lighthouse of sorts. No matter the conditions, these words guide us home. A line from that manifesto kept popping into my head: *We believe in human kindness, knowing we are made better when we work together.*

What opportunities to treat people with kindness had I missed? Maybe the implications weren't always so dire, but where could I have tipped the dominos, so to speak, if I had only stopped to consider it? So many times it's not that people don't care to be kind; it's that life is moving too quickly for us to stop and think about how an outpouring of kindness could start. We're hurrying home to make dinner, we're late to pick up the kids from practice, we're swamped at work, we're stuck in traffic. Any thought given to someone else (and how we might change their day for good) gets buried under the noise and stressors of what we have going on in our own lives.

I didn't want to get tangled up in the shouting match about gun control and mental health issues, but I knew I had to do something. It occurred to me: What good is this network I've built if I don't rely on it.. *right now?* Still, Jo and I realized that using our platform would only go so far. We needed to involve more people, knowing that true power is not in the "me" but in the "we."

I wanted to work through this with the people around me—a process I've always found helpful—so Jo and I rallied the Magnolia team together to hear their thoughts. We all came to the conclusion that the challenge was right in front of us: make kindness louder.

Louder than chaos.

Louder than hate.

I'm not talking about kindness in terms of grand gestures or the goodwill that comes on special occasions or holidays. I'm talking about day-to-day interactions that offer a glimmer of love or hope. The kind of goodness that abounds in equal measure for a loved one and a stranger on the street, people on both sides of our bubbles. That's the kind of kindness that can tip the dominos in the opposite direction.

A subtle reminder is sometimes all it takes. A nudge to do just one small thing. At Magnolia we made up four fliers with pull-tabs suggesting practical ways to show kindness. We shared them on social media so people could print them out and also offer this idea to those in their own networks. Two of the flyer templates had general acts of kindness, those you could use around the home or office. The third flyer was geared toward kids, and the fourth was blank, which we hoped would empower people to think of even more ways to help.

Mow a neighbor's lawn.
Write a letter of thanks to a first responder.
Stop and ask a person experiencing homelessness their story.

We knew we weren't reinventing the wheel, but we hoped that something tangible—that little slip of paper—might burn a hole in someone's pocket until they decided to act on it.

Within hours, the post took off. People all over the world downloaded the flyers, and we were blown away by the responses and stories that people sent in using the hashtag #makekindnessloud.

That's it. That's the stuff. Real and important change begins with small, courageous acts.

KINDNESS FLYER

Make your own kindness flyer for your fridge to remind you to perform random acts of kindness. Make a practice of pulling off a tab any time you feel a kindness deficit in the world. Here are a few ideas to get you started:

- Buy coffee for the person behind you in line at the coffee shop.
- Make time to call a friend.
- Ask a stranger how they're doing.
- Write a thank-you note to a former boss or teacher.
- Volunteer at a local charity.
- Tell someone what you like best about them.

GET UNCOMFORTABLY KIND

We tend to think that kindness is easy. Soft. *Nice.* It's something you learn in kindergarten—how to say "please" and "thank you" and share your Goldfish crackers. Kindness has gotten a rep of being like Glinda the Good Witch, all gentleness and smiles. Someone with a "No, please, after you, I insist" type attitude. It's easy to think, *That's just not me. I'm not a pushover, I'm not constantly in a good mood, and I'm not always patient and nice.* But real kindness is built with grace and grit, and I don't think one works without the other; they are wisely intertwined. Because life-changing kindness is *hard.* Sometimes so hard it hurts. It's sweat and effort. It actually requires something of you. That's kindness that inspires, kindness that makes a difference.

In the story of the widow's mite in the Bible,[3] Jesus watched at the temple in silence as rich men made donations—some of them quite large—into the treasury. But then a poor widow placed two small copper coins in the box, barely a fraction of a penny. That was when Jesus spoke up, saying that this woman had given more than any of the others, even the richest of them, because she had made a true sacrifice.

How many times have you stopped short of giving because it would require something slightly inconvenient to you, maybe something as small as creating an account and a password to donate to a worthy cause?

Ninety-nine percent of kindness, of generosity, of fairness, of justice is follow-through. It requires sacrifice. It is *uncomfortable.* You hold the door for an older person on their way out of the grocery store—that's kind—but when you help load their groceries into their car, even though you're already running late, that's uncomfortably kind. A teacher who gives a struggling student an extra-credit opportunity—that's kind. Coming in early every day to go over her lessons is uncomfortably kind. If we are going to belong to one another again, we need to get comfortable with being uncomfortably kind.

During the recent protests surrounding the Black Lives Matter movement, a local woman tweeted at me. In a totally nonconfrontational way she asked if Magnolia would consider making a percentage of our vendors at our upcoming vendor fair Black-owned businesses. It took about two seconds for me to say yes. That part was a cinch. That was easy kind. The hard part, the uncomfortable part, was following through by doing our due diligence to find and invite vendors in an honorable way, and making sure their businesses wouldn't be overwhelmed by the bump in volume that could come. It made more work for our staff, but it was worth it a thousandfold. Society would have us believe that we have to be cutthroat to excel in business and in life, but I've learned to place my bets on a different theory: kindness never returns void.

When we push the borders of the bubble far enough, it eventually bursts. That's when we can see what has been true all along—there is no difference in worthiness between those inside the bubble and those outside. We all belong to one another, and there's no good reason why kindness shouldn't blanket and protect us all. It's like the old Irish proverb that says, "It is in the shelter of each other that the people live."

If we are going to belong to one another again, we need to get comfortable with being uncomfortably kind. #makesense

I read a great story that illustrates what can happen when you break through your bubble. In early 2020, Qasim Rashid was running for Congress in Virginia. As he was campaigning he received a lot of support, but he was also on the butt end of a lot of upsetting anti-Muslim comments. One day, a guy named Oscar Dillon blasted out a tweet, the gist of which was that Rashid was not welcome in America.

Anyone who has ever been on the internet knows how these exchanges usually go down—someone says something incendiary, then someone who disagrees either makes an impassioned argument or they hit back with bombs lobbed at the opposition, which usually just results in more name-calling and spite. Rashid took a different tack. He did a little research and saw that Dillon was having medical issues and had set up a GoFundMe to pay for his mounting bills. Dillon had absolutely gutted his retirement savings and was now having to dip into his wife's savings to cover the costs. When Rashid saw that, instead of firing back at Dillon, he took a risk. He set aside his own hurt, gave up his own affronted dignity, and decided to get uncomfortably kind. He donated to the GoFundMe—and then encouraged his supporters to do the same. Within weeks, the campaign was up to $20,000.

Dillon watched donations racking up, just staring at his screen in shock. He couldn't believe that Rashid had reached out to take his hand given the way he'd treated him. He asked Rashid to meet, and when they did, they spoke openly to each other, and Dillon apologized for his tweet. Not only that, he invited Rashid to put campaign signs in his yard![4]

When Rashid made the choice to see Dillon as a person, to look at his life as a whole, to understand where he might be coming from, it made all the difference. I genuinely believe that the more we operate in this kind of mindset, believing the best about people, the more likely it is that those people will believe the same in others. That's another thing about kindness: it's contagious.

I still believe, as I did that horrible Sunday in 2019, that our collective kindness can become louder than any individual acts of hate. But that's only if we don't let ourselves go numb. Only if we expand our bubbles until they disappear. If we ask the hard questions. *What pain does the world have that causes me to ache? What small thing can I do about it today?* Maybe in that process you help someone who was so lost they were headed down a path that would have been destructive to themselves or to a whole bunch of people. We must build up instead of tearing down. So much of what we know is broken. The way we treat our neighbors. How we speak to one another. And we have to start moving back to a place of love and civility. A place of concern and respect. Jo and I want to operate with the kind of love and kindness that lends itself to rolling up our sleeves and working hard. If we're doing it right, we're all in the restoration business.

Kindness asks us to look each other in the eye and see one another as valuable human beings. This begins at home, in our own networks and communities, with a steadfast belief that we are made better when we believe the best about each other.

Acts of kindness often occur in the absence of witnesses. We also can't always see the immediate effect. But rest assured, if the conditions are right, kindness moves and shifts like wildfire, and its beauty lies in its potential to spread. To catalyze a series of reactions that can transform how we care for one another.

The spark has to begin somewhere. Let it begin with you.

BOTTOM LINE

Real impact happens when we give something of ourselves.

CHAPTER 7

MY NETWORK: MY FAMILY

My earliest network was my family. These are the folks who built me. Different as we were, their unwavering belief in who I was became the major runway of my life. It gave me a foundation so firm that I didn't have to think twice when it came to dreaming big and taking risks. Their love and support taught me the importance of having people in your network who are there to cheer you on every step of the way.

—Chip

GAYLE / CHIP'S MOM

One of my favorite photos from Chip's childhood was taken of him at day care. In many ways, it says it all. I'm betting he was three or four at the time. All of his classmates stood around him, and smack in the middle was Chip, his arms crossed, a smile stretching from ear to ear. Chip loved day care. He couldn't wait to go bursting through the doors every morning to see his friends. Even then he had charisma and confidence that made him a natural leader. And when you paired that leadership with his deep love for people, it was pretty special.

In listening to him talk about this book, I was reminded of our neighborhood back in New Mexico, before we moved to Texas. I'd be driving home from somewhere and would come around the corner to see all these kids running down our street. One of them was always out front—Chip. Even at a young age, Chip had a maturity about him. I don't know how to say it other than he had a magnetic personality. Back then, when he was just three feet tall, he was already making real connections with people, even if it was just the kids on our block. He was bold but kind, and others naturally followed him.

I liked to write letters to my kids when they were young. Here's one I wrote for Chip when he was about eight years old:

> Chip, what an honor it is to be your mother. I
> want to tell you about some of the gifts God has
> given you. First of all, you are cool. Like Fonzie
> is cool. You have a way of letting your friends
> know you're the leader. But you know, God gives
> you talents and He expects you to use them for
> Him. Because you will be a leader you must learn
> to set yourself apart.

Even as a kid, Chip reminded me of King David in the Bible— strong but soft-hearted. I knew that my son would be good at most everything he tried, but I reminded him often to keep his focus on a higher purpose.

The reason I mention the importance of having that higher purpose is that from his earliest days we knew Chip was different from the others. He could draw people to him. A quality like that could be used for good, but it could also be used for bad.

Raising Chip wasn't always roses. I was constantly being called to the school for teacher meetings about his grades. He'd be failing math or science, or something like that, and I'd go in to talk with the teacher while Chip would be outside throwing the football, happy as a lark. I guess he knew that I'd come out with some extra homework, and then he'd do whatever additional assignment was given to him to pull his grade up.

Chip always had stuff going on in his head. He had more ideas than he could keep up with, let's put it that way. But he never wasted a lot of worry on things he didn't think really mattered, not the way other kids might have. He was kind of like Tom Sawyer.

It might not have always been evident in the classroom, but Chip has never shied away from hard work. Bob and I were adamant that work would be the fabric of our household. But not every child takes to work like Chip did. Every chance we got, our kids were out in the yard with us, pulling weeds or doing some kind of chore. There was always a lesson in it and sometimes even a reward—an ice cream at the end of a long, hot day of mowing the lawn.

Recently, I found an old picture Chip had drawn with crayon shortly after we moved from New Mexico to Texas. He was in third grade. It was a pretty hard transition for him, particularly since he'd had to leave his best friend behind. In the drawing there was a house that was decorated with Christmas lights. The sun was shining, and there was an apple tree and flowers out front. This was the caption:

Well, it's hard to move, but after we are finished decorating, I think I will like it better.

It hit me, years later, that maybe this was God hinting at Joanna's presence in Chip's life. The life they would start together, the multiple hard moves they would have, and the role she would play. Chip would build the house, and Jo would make it home.

As a parent, one thing I always wanted Chip to feel was love and support. There was hardly an event he participated in or a sport he played that we missed. Being there for him was important to us as parents, and we wanted him to know that by our actions, not just our words.

We were there to support him later on, too, when the stakes were higher. When he and Jo first started buying and renovating houses, they got to a point where they needed help. They needed money to make these projects happen. And even though we weren't always convinced it was the best investment we could make, when asked we helped with all we could. The thing about Chip was that he was never afraid of failing. He would always rather fail than not try something. Bob and I, on the other hand, never had the guts to gamble like Chip did.

What Chip and Jo did took guts, but it also took support. You talk about a network—what's the first part of that? *Net.* I think Chip knew he could rely on Bob and me to help be his "net." I hope that knowing that made a difference in the choices and the risks he was willing to make.

During his last year of high school, some of the awards Chip received summed up the kind of teenager he was: "Class Favorite," "Most Flirtatious," and the one I was most proud of—"Best Leader."

I guess I was right about the leadership part all those years before when he was in preschool. That aspect of his character continued to grow with him. I think I said it best in a letter I wrote to him his junior year of high school:

You never cease to amaze me with your ability to read people, your insight, your desire to please God, your dad and I, and your love of people.

Darn it, you aren't that cute little red-haired boy with the cars on his underwear who was all over the neighborhood with his buddy, but you are more awesome than ever.

Thanks for being my friend and more than that, my son of whom I am well pleased.

Love,

Mom

BOB / CHIP'S DAD

The earliest foundation Chip and I had was built on sports. I played college football and dreamed that would be the sport my son would excel in, but Chip gravitated more toward baseball. Getting the chance to play in the big leagues was our head-down goal together. Chip showed great grit. He might not have had my speed or height, but he had determination, and his work ethic was tireless.

I remember seeing Chip out in the backyard, in August, in the *blazing* Texas heat, throwing baseballs through a tire because the team needed him as pitcher. Pitching wasn't necessarily his strength, but he was going to do everything in his power to succeed in it. That was his nature—to give his best to whatever situation he was in.

These traits were pretty evident in the way he carried himself with his teammates, too, so it was little wonder that even though baseball was his strongest sport, he was voted captain of the football team as well.

No matter what sport it was, playing it well was our push, and it became the vehicle that connected us. I got to teach, and Chip got to learn. I coached him on the field. I coached him off the field. That's basically how our whole world turned.

My favorite memory of those thousands of hours spent on the field came during Chip's junior year. We were playing in a tournament in Arlington, a neighboring city, and our high school team was playing a pretty powerful baseball school. Longtime major-leaguer Tom Grieve had a son, Ben (who went on to nine years in the big leagues), who was playing there at the time. Chip had an unbelievable tournament. Every time he got up, he got a hit. I think he hit over .500 that weekend. His focus was just through the roof. I sat up in the stands thinking, *Wow. Chip has turned the corner here.* That kind of play could get him noticed. He could be drafted and even get a top scholarship.

Chip's team ended up winning that tournament, and Chip made the All-Tournament Team. I think he might have even been named Most Valuable Player. That next year, we won our district and then went pretty far in the playoffs. It was a fun time. We ended up getting a bunch of local people to help pay for an airplane to fly us down to El Paso to play a team there. We didn't win, but the whole experience felt like a first step toward the big leagues, just like we'd always dreamed.

But there was another reality that came from all that work we did together. When your dad is your coach, you kind of get robbed of having that advocate who can help you get the attention of schools for scholarships. What dad doesn't say, "My son is awesome"? So when it came time to reach out to schools, I was limited in how effective I could be in promoting Chip. Because I had always been his coach, he didn't have other strong voices out there making calls for him.

Chip ended up at a junior college and then chose to transfer to play at Baylor, where the coach offered him a walk-on opportunity.

Being a walk-on is tough. You have to pay your own way to school to play for the team. Big schools like Baylor invite a number of players to walk on, and they have to fight for playing time. The situation got tougher for Chip because right after he agreed to go to Baylor, the long-time coach resigned, and a new guy came in. So now he had to impress someone who wasn't even the coach who thought enough of him to bring him on. Giving up would have made sense to most people, but Chip didn't, and for that I was really proud of him.

There's a story Chip told me not long after he transferred to Baylor. After a few practices the team held a scrimmage, which was his chance to distinguish himself among the other players and show the new Baylor coach what he could do.

Things were going okay. Chip hit a single off of this talented pitcher out of Dallas. Then Chip did what he always did—he took a lead off first, looking like he might steal second. But the pitcher did this pick-off move that Chip had never seen before. Chip got caught in the base path—and he was out.

The scrimmage went on, and Chip did it again—another hit and another pick-off at first.

Then it happened a *third* time. If I'd been there that day, I would've pulled my hair out. I get why the coach was mad. I would've been mad, too, but looking back, it showed Chip had guts. If he saw an opportunity, he was going to take it—regardless of the risk. And if the outcome he got was bad, well, he wasn't afraid to try again.. and again.

Chip didn't end up making that Baylor team, but it took several days for him to get up the courage to call and tell me. It wasn't until years later that I realized the agony he went through in making that call. He thought I'd be angry or heartbroken or something in between.

And he was right. Chip's decision to stop playing ball felt like a personal loss. My mindset was always about winning. I took the whole Churchill mentality to the extreme—*don't ever, ever quit.* I'm so hard-headed that I couldn't see that sometimes in insisting on going forward, you're actually going backward. When Chip said that he was done with baseball—that he wasn't going to leave Baylor to transfer to another team—I couldn't imagine what would be next for him. I saw that as giving up on a dream—the dream we'd both had for his whole life.

But over the years, as I've watched Chip as a father and the way he interacts with his own kids in their sports, I see that he was built differently than me. He's still competitive, but he's more laid-back, more focused on encouraging those kids to believe that nothing is impossible.

As Gayle was going through old notes from us, we found this one I'd typed out on our old typewriter for Chip's fifteenth birthday:

```
Chip, I need you to believe in yourself like I
believe in you. There is nothing you cannot
accomplish when you put your mind to it.
```

When I wrote that back then, I didn't know the half of it. I had no idea where the next thirty years would lead him and what he would accomplish.

In the early days I got a front-row seat to Chip's determination and resilience. And now the world gets to see it. Those qualities have taken him so much further than any baseball diamond ever could.

SHANNON / CHIP'S SISTER

You could say my little brother and I are complete opposites. I'm very Type A, and Chip is, well.. *not*. I like my stuff all in one place, so that was always an issue. When we were growing up, I knew the very instant I walked into my room if Chip had been in there messing with my stuff. I could tell if there was even one paper out of place.

It was typical sibling rivalry. I'd tattle on him at the dinner table. "Dad, Chip almost shot Magic with your gun today." (Magic was our dog, and it was totally an accident.)

But as different as we were, and still are, Chip and I have similar qualities. We're both athletic, and we both *live* for competition. As kids, we'd field balls with Dad together any chance we could.

We were also both pretty funny. We laughed so much in our family, especially about the disasters that seemed to always happen on family trips. The camper would have a flat tire or Dad would do something like drop all the food on the ground, and after we got over the shock of it, we'd all start laughing. That was how we processed things—with humor.

As much as Chip and I were encouraged to work in athletics, we were also encouraged to work at home. And when we'd complain that we didn't have enough time in the day for all of it—our jobs, our chores, our sports practice, and then the extra practice Dad would have us do after that—my dad's response was always the same: "Well, you always have time at 4:00 a.m." Maybe that's why to this day Chip is such an early riser.

Working was just a thing in our family. We didn't complain about it. We honestly didn't mind it too much. We made money. We had something to do. And keeping busy making money was a pretty good combination. Chip and I sold Dad's lapel pins from his sporting goods store and Mom's chocolate-chip cookies at the state basketball tournaments. We set up a business to collect and discard old Christmas trees and took them to be mulched. (I think we got a whole twelve dollars apiece for them.) If there was a creative idea to make money, we were in.

Our family always had a unified front on these crazy business ventures. One time Mom and Dad took us out of school for a week to go to a big sports event and we sold sporting equipment out of our little pop-up camper. It was our family bonding. It's just what we did.

Years later, with my own family, I've carried on the legacy of placing a big emphasis on sports. Both of my children were college athletes, and my husband and I live for going to the games.

But Chip has carried on the tradition of serial business ideas. That was *always* his fascination. I remember one time going to Six Flags and looking over to see Chip quizzing the guy running some booth. *How much is your rent on this? How much does your inventory cost? What can you sell on a busy day?*

We'd be waiting to ride the rides, and Chip would be fantasizing about making money at a theme park.

Chip carried that curiosity about how to capitalize for years. When George W. Bush and Dick Cheney won the presidential election in what had been an insanely close race with Al Gore and Joe Lieberman, Chip was in college and, seemingly overnight, had T-shirts printed that said "Sore Loserman." As you might imagine, in Waco, Texas, he was selling them like hotcakes.

Chip was definitely the golden child, which was always a little annoying for me as the older sister, but there was good reason for it. Chip really does have a heart of gold, and he has since he was small. We'd be watching some show and an infomercial would come on about orphans in Africa; before I knew it, he would have donated all of his money to them—the money he'd spent weeks figuring out how to earn.

But that's Chip. Besides compassion, his greatest strength is his optimism. It's like a magnet that draws people to him. They want a cheerleader. They love to hear, "You can do this." That's always been Chip's way of talking to people, because it's always been his way of seeing things. He speaks with optimism, and he believes it.

Watching Chip's success over the years has proven to me that the world is hungry not just for someone positive but for normal, authentic, down-to-earth people. And my brother is just that. Truly, he and Jo are the salt of the earth.

When he told me that he was writing a book about building a network, he might have expected that I would poke fun or make one of my usual teasing remarks. *You already wrote a book, dummy.*

But I'm a truth teller. I always have been. So instead I said, "That's the perfect topic for you, Chip. You've been building your network your whole life."

MY NETWORK: JOANNA'S FAMILY

My family in-law is living proof of the power of growing your network. Joanna's family is supremely special. There are few better human beings on the planet. Before I became part of their family, I admired their closeness. You could tell, just by watching them, how fiercely protective they are of one another. They have shown me over and over again what it looks like to be there for the people in your network, and I'm honored that somewhere along the way I've been able to show them the thrill that comes with taking risks and reaching for a life that truly lights you up.

—Chip

MRS. STEVENS / CHIP'S MOTHER-IN-LAW

We have prayed for Joanna since before we brought her home from the hospital as a little baby. We prayed for her friends, her career, and the man she would one day marry. We have three daughters, and we prayed these things for each of them. That may sound strange to some people, but I think most parents, even if they are not praying about it, can't help but dream about what their children's lives are going to look like. Oftentimes the reality ends up being very different from what you envisioned.

As Joanna started to grow up, I imagined the type of man she'd marry. I pictured someone in a suit and tie, a Wall Street type. Joanna always loved New York.

She was also very steady, like her father. I've always said those two are like a pair of oak trees. Of all our daughters, Joanna was the most shy. She was beautiful and social, but not very interested in guys. She didn't date a lot. So I was surprised the day Joanna told me she had met a boy at her father's Firestone shop, and that she might go out with him.

"What did he look like?" I asked.

She shrugged.

"Was he tall or short? Blond hair..?"

"I don't remember," she said. "His name is Chip."

Joanna had had a long conversation with this boy, Chip, but she couldn't remember what he looked like!

Jerry and I didn't have to wait long to find out for ourselves what he looked like because the very next day he came back into the Firestone shop. We were standing behind the sales counter and Chip came in wearing shorts with boots and these tall white socks. He walked over to us and asked if he could take Joanna out on a date. My husband remembers Chip was eating some kind of candy, and it had gotten stuck in his teeth, so he had his finger in his mouth, trying to get it out. All of the sales guys were just staring at him, but Chip didn't seem to care one bit.

Now that I know Chip, it makes sense why Jo's memory of him

What I remember looking like   What Mrs. Stevens remembers

was hazy. He is like a ball of energy. His personality is bigger than his physical appearance. The connection Joanna felt with him when they first met must have been a sign that there was something deeper at work.

Chip was not in any way what we were expecting that day, but I was impressed that he'd done the proper thing and thought to ask us if he could take our daughter out on a date. As parents, we would have fought it if it felt wrong, but for some reason we gave him our blessing. Our hearts weren't anxious. I think that's because we could already tell that Chip's heart was good.

As their dating became more serious, Joanna brought him around our family more often. He was very comfortable with us, and I started to see how funny Chip was. I like to be funny too. I do stupid things and laugh at myself, but Chip was different. He was so bold. I remember one time he called out our family photographs on the wall.

"You all have black clothes on," he said. "Where was this taken? A funeral? Y'all are so serious."

exhibit A: Jo's family   exhibit B: My family

(What you can't tell is that we're all
wearing different shades of pink.)

That was a pretty brave comment to make to your new girlfriend's family, but he was kind of right. "We were on a family vacation," I told him, and we all laughed.

He was also crazy about Joanna and very affectionate. My husband and I fell in love through letters we wrote to each other, so our relationship involved distance and patience. But there was an intimacy to our daughter's relationship with Chip. A physical closeness that took some getting used to. He wasn't inappropriate, just really affectionate, taking every chance he got to put his arm around her.

We would have Chip over for dinner, and really, we had never seen anything like it. Granted we've been married forty-eight years, but my husband is not a touchy person. We hold hands, but that's usually the extent of it publicly. Joanna, like her dad, is also not a touchy person. So someone coming into our home and being so overly affectionate with her was strange. I laugh now, but at the time I was like, "My gosh, leave that girl alone!"

But we always trusted Joanna's judgment. She never had a curfew because there was no need for one. If she was ever late, she called. She was so wise and self-assured.

When it was clear she was falling in love with Chip we knew there was something special about him. Yet we weren't totally without reservations. We saw a restlessness in Chip, which can sometimes be a very negative thing. He hadn't discovered himself yet. I didn't worry too much, because I could see how much he wanted to find his own way. He was really searching. That searching would lead them to endure some hard things as a couple.

Early on, as they were growing their business, there were times when they were struggling financially. We had no idea how bad it was for them during those early years until we read about it in their first book. (As close as we are, Joanna has always been one not to want to worry her parents.) But now, it also makes me glad in a way. Because they went through that journey, they are now able to understand other people's hard journeys too. As a mother, my heart ached for them, but I know God has used that hardship for good.

The show of course had some positive implications, but when it ended, we were actually excited. We could tell it was time for them to take a step back. They were killing themselves. They were worn out. As their parents, we saw the piranhas all around, wanting a little piece of them. And for Chip, you can't put him in a little glass box and say, "You have to act like this." He wasn't able to fully be himself, and the fun had started to fade. Today, they still have enormous pressures—even more than before—but there's more freedom now.

I like to look at things from a nontraditional angle. That's where Chip and I are alike. Actually, Chip is multilevel in his approach. And while most corporate executives, when they do strength assessments, fit into one level, Chip has a lot of extra gifts. For instance, people who talk a lot are not often great listeners. That is how some people can underestimate Chip. He does talk a lot, but he listens too.

Chip is also always about the other person, not himself. For example, we never really knew that Joanna was creative. She had a God-given gift, of course, but the full capacity of that never really came out until Chip encouraged it. He drew it out of her, and he does the same for other people. He brings out the best in them. He's that same way with his kids. I have always said, "I wish I had a dad like him." I am so thankful that my grandchildren get to experience him as a father.

One day, after Chip and Jo had been married for a few years, I was having my morning devotional and praying for all of my children. As I started praying for Chip, suddenly the Lord showed me this big, wide-open space, like Montana or Wyoming. There were green hills, and this beautiful mustang was right there in the middle of a field, all by itself. It was just running all over the place, wild and free. But still searching. I told my husband about the vision. "Chip is like a mustang. There's a wildness in him, but it's okay.. it's who the Lord created him to be."

Chip wasn't the picture of steady that we'd envisioned for our daughter, but he was always sure about the things that mattered. He was learning to be confident in who he was and who he wasn't. And his love for Joanna and his children has never wavered.

JERRY / CHIP'S FATHER-IN-LAW

I will never forget the day I met Chip Gaines. He came strolling into the Firestone shop—a big presence, right down to his cowboy boots and tube socks.

He was coming to ask us if he could take Joanna out. For my wife, that was a big check mark in her book. But for me, there were no check marks that day. Well, except maybe one—in the box that said No Way.

The more we got to know Chip, the more we realized that, well.. he was different. He definitely marched to the beat of his own drum, but my wife and I were keeping an open mind. I never prayed for any of my future sons-in-law to be rich, but I always hoped and expected that they would have secure jobs so they could take care of our daughters.

Once Jo and Chip started going out regularly, I realized this guy was anything but financially steady. He was dabbling and trying all kinds of things. He was doing yards; he had the wash-n-fold and a firecracker stand. It was pretty obvious that a suit and tie was not going to be his thing.

One thing I never doubted was that Chip was an entrepreneur at heart. He always had great thoughts and ideas and could really think outside the box. But once he got a thing started, he needed somebody to help him manage it, to handle the day-to-day stuff. 'Cause Chip was already off looking for the next deal.

Even early on when we were a little uncertain about him, we were impressed by Chip's circle of friends. He surrounded himself with a good group of people. He was running with guys who had good heads on their shoulders. Though from the outside, they seemed the total opposite of him. I mean, Chip would carry every last dollar he had to his name in the right pocket of his jeans. (Which, my wife was always noting, constantly had holes in them.) He didn't even have a bank account.

But like the saying "Water seeks its own level," Chip was always finding people who, on the inside, were on the same level of character, which is something he's continued to do as his circle has grown.

Because Chip was trustworthy and made people feel comfortable, he was a natural salesman. I always said he'd make a terrific car salesman, but he had no interest in that. Since I worked for Firestone, I set him up with a job interview with Hunter Engineering. I knew Chip could talk to people, so I thought he could sell tire balances and that kind of thing. "You could do some traveling, meet some people.." I tried to entice him.

He took the interview, but it didn't work out. My guess is he just tanked it because he wasn't interested. Still, I kept trying to help him with his career, asking him to go on business trips with me—day trips to check on customers. Chip is naturally very inquisitive, so there was always something for him to ask about and learn, even in tire shops. And I liked our time in the car because I genuinely wanted to get to know him better. We'd ride together and I'd nonchalantly ask about his work and the houses he was redoing, but it seemed he and Jo were in over their heads. Nothing seemed secure, even the vehicle he drove. (He had this old beat-up truck that my guys at the shop were always having to fix.)

A few times when we were alone together, I'd even be so bold as to say things directly, like, "Haven't you gotten a job yet?"

On one of these trips, after a couple of years of this, Chip snapped back very matter-of-factly, "I have a job."

And for some reason, at that moment, it clicked with me. I might not understand it, it might not be my way of doing things, but this was what he considered work, and I needed to shut up about it.

And that was that. I never asked him again, even though a few times I might've wanted to. I knew Chip was always going to be looking for the next deal. You couldn't tie him down. He was a mustang, just like my wife said.

Fast-forward to today, and I'm technically on Chip's payroll. I questioned his house flipping as a career (or even as a sound investment), but a few years later, he actually advised me on buying a commercial property. It was a pretty big deal for me from a financial standpoint, and I knew I needed counsel from someone with insight. Chip is great at negotiations. He knows how to price properties and knows how to get a good deal. So I knew I wanted to meet with him to get his advice.

I gave Chip my proposal, and when I was finished, his initial reaction was to talk me out of it. "Just be careful," he said.

I told him that I'd done the research and I thought it was a really good investment.

"Well, okay, if you think it's a good deal. Go for it," he finally said.

So I did—and after it was all said and done, I told my wife, "Wow.

That was fun. Now I know why he does what he does." My inspiration, and my willingness to take the risk, all came from Chip.

I found out later that it meant a lot to Chip that I sought his advice. It was a full-circle moment, not just for him, but for both of us. So much of his behavior I had formerly thought was foolishness. I used to say things like, "How do you know it's $25,000 worth of work? You don't know what's behind the walls.." I'd tell him he needed to carry a notepad and pen to bid sites, to look more professional. Things like that.

I always thought he was just a gambler, but when I came to work for him, I realized he has a brilliant business mind. But if you asked me how he and Jo got to where they are today, I wouldn't say it's because of his mind. I'd say it's because of his heart.

Chip would do anything for anybody. He's not judgmental. He doesn't preach—he walks. I remember this one time I hired a guy who'd been down on his luck to mow my lawn. When he got to our house, it was obvious that he had no idea what he was doing. Chip saw this and ran out and bought the guy a self-propelled mower so he could at least have a chance at succeeding. A few weeks later, we saw the mower for sale at a pawn shop. But it didn't bother Chip. That's just his heart. He sees a need and he'll do anything he can to fulfill it. He and Jo never tell us the things they do for people nowadays, but we hear from others about their phenomenal generosity.

Chip has taught us that sometimes the prayers we hope for arrive in different packaging, but that doesn't make them less than what we had asked for. In this case, they were even greater.

MARY KAY / CHIP'S SISTER-IN-LAW

I don't remember my big sister ever going on dates, so when she told me she was going out with this guy named Chip, I was pretty excited to help her get ready for the big night. I don't remember what time he was supposed to arrive, but I do know that time came and went. And then another hour passed. And another. I'd already decided I didn't like him, even before we'd met.

When Chip did eventually show up, he walked in wearing this brown-orange suede leather jacket, and he really was just *so* loud. Immediately I was like, *Whoa, you're too much*. I didn't expect there to be a second date.

Obviously we know there was. Pretty quickly Chip started coming around more and more, often joining our family for dinner. It was around our dinner table that I started to see how capable he was of changing the fabric of our family—for the better. Typically, family dinners were quiet. It's not that we didn't have a lot to say to one another; we're just a more reserved group. But when Chip showed up, our dinner table was *alive*. He was always asking questions and really engaging with everyone. He took our steady, calm vibe and rocked the boat. At first, that made me nervous. There was so much I admired about my big sissy. She was diligent and faithful. She was such a consistent figure in my life, and I remember thinking, *I don't want this guy changing her*. But that's what has always been so magnetic about Chip and Jo. They are each other's counterpoint. What each of them was lacking they found in the other.

Chip has such a unique curiosity about what life has to offer. He always seemed so swept up by possibility and really showed a heart for wanting to live the best life he could. He doesn't like complacency, and if he sees the people he loves settling, he's not going to be quiet about it.

When I was dating my now-husband, David, I realized how much Chip wants those same things for everyone. He has always showed up for us and been there to push us toward the risks worth taking. He's encouraged David and me to be brave and to fight for the things that matter to us.

Yes, Chip is (still) loud. Yes, he'll talk forever. But it won't be about him. He is hilarious and goofy and witty, and that's what most people see. But the lucky few also get to see that he's equally intentional and purposeful and deep. His heart for pushing others to be their best selves has forever changed our family.

TERESA / CHIP'S SISTER-IN-LAW

I honestly can't remember meeting Chip for the first time. I guess you could call it the "Chip effect." It's like an anomaly where your mind convinces you that you've known him your entire life. When my husband and I met him, he wasn't a stranger. He was already family. For instance, when Chip speaks and is engaged in conversation, there is intentionality. There is purpose. So being that we hadn't met him in person before, his ability to connect was incredibly considerate—as if we were picking up right where we had left off.

With all that said, no matter what is going on in life, whether good, bad, or indifferent, he sees a seemingly ordinary moment as unique and crucial. He makes them significant opportunities: either a learning tool, a learning lesson, or a means to help other people along the way.

There's one moment in particular that I will remember for the rest of my life. After Chip and Jojo had been married for a few years, my husband and I and our family came to Texas from Michigan for a visit. We all managed to get into this large conversion van one morning to go out to breakfast. As we were all talking, with no warning, the van suddenly stopped moving. We had gone from about forty miles per hour to a sudden stop in seconds. Chip placed the van in park and jumped out. We didn't know what happened until Jojo said, "Aww, he's been looking for James for a couple weeks."

Come to find out, James was homeless and Chip had been looking for him, hoping to get him a winter coat and blanket. I watched Chip jog a bit after him. You could tell he was calling out his name as James finally stopped and turned around. Chip caught up to him, placing his arm around this big man. He walked right alongside him like he was with a friend, going on a walk. They exchanged a few words, and what looked like money, shook each other's hand, and gave a quick hug as Chip made it back to the van. As he jumped back in, he put it in drive. We didn't talk about it. Instead, Chip carried on with the conversation we'd been having as though nothing had ever happened.

This is who Chip is. Who I know he was meant to be. He's a miner. He sees the hard stuff as a place to plant his feet on solid ground. It's as if he has this rare, really good fear that reminds him, "This moment may not come around again in your lifetime," and so he seizes it. My sister is proof of that. He knew she was rare in the most beautiful way.

What I've grown to realize about Chip is this: He is tame yet untamable. Carefree but not careless. And whenever you encounter him, he leaves you with this assurance that you have the power to live out who you are meant to be.

CHAPTER 9

TYING TIES

Years ago Jo and I were out to dinner at this little bed-and-breakfast on the outskirts of town that had just started opening up to the public for meals. As the sun went down the restaurant was like a beehive buzzing with activity—chefs calling out orders and busboys turning tables as quickly as their hands could move. As our server came by to hand us our menus, I noticed she had a tattoo of the Jolly Roger on the inside of her wrist. I was dying to know how on earth a Pirates fan ended up working in a B&B in Texas, so I asked her about it.

A few minutes after we'd ordered, I looked out the window and saw a gentleman in a pair of ironed blue jeans step out of a truck that had a Keenan Engineering decal on the side. I popped up for a second and went over to talk to him at the hostess stand. Turned out he was new in town, just moved to Texas from Arizona, and was starting up a business doing home inspections. I already had a lot of home inspectors I trusted, but I took his card and slipped it in my back pocket.

I came back to find our food had come while I was up, but as I sat down I couldn't help but overhear that the couple at the table next to us was visiting Baylor with their daughter. They were trying to decide if it was the right school for her. Of course I had to tell them that was my alma mater they were talking about, and that I'd be more than happy to answer any questions they had—as long as they weren't about academics. I lifted my fork to dig in to my food and looked over at Jo. She was giving me a look that I know quite well, a look that said, *Are you done yet?*

It's a couple decades later and I still have that same focus to engage and connect. For me, this is what networking is all about—making a genuine connection, one that starts at the heart and has no destination in mind other than *closer*.

I have always known that we are all part of one giant cloth. A bunch of threads, one tapestry. It's almost like I can see the stitches floating between us, holding us together. That invisible web of connection feels to me like something beautiful, something bigger than us. Those connections are always there, waiting for us to tighten them.

I might have been born with the talkative gene, but it was my mom who raised me to be a *radical connector*. For those who know anything about my mother, the idea of her encouraging me to be a radical *anything* might draw a laugh. She is a very traditional woman. When she married my dad in 1970 and they moved to Albuquerque, the Summer of Love was still in full swing all around her. Her head just about exploded with everyone burning their bras and flying their freak flags. There she was, an Elvis Presley fan in a poodle skirt, while the rest of the world was already onto Birkenstocks and Beatlemania. She doesn't exactly scream "maverick" in her tucked-in blouse, but in this one particular way, she is as radical as anyone on the planet. Early on she saw—really saw—who I was. I was a kid who reached out to anyone and everyone to get to know them a little better. That wasn't necessarily how she herself had grown up, but she saw that in my nature and insisted I follow my heart.

I've always had confidence that if I approached with sincere interest, people would respond. When I was in my twenties, I read the famous Dale Carnegie quote that says, "You can make more friends in two months by becoming interested in other people than you can in two years by trying to get other people interested in you."[1] I knew how true that was because my mom had let me figure it out for myself.

Because of my mom's openness, even as a kid I made a habit out of making the rounds. I didn't just hang with my crew day in and day out; I had friends in every group. If someone were to make a movie about my high school years, in the opening scene the camera would pan the cafeteria, showing groups of kids clustered together in little islands of sameness. There'd be the real studious kids with their noses in books at one table, the drama kids hamming it up at another, the goths ruminating at another, and since we were in Texas, the ropers in their cowboy boots at another. Finally, you'd land on the table where I was, the jock table. We were a bunch of A Team–looking kids who carried some of the swagger of the football field or the baseball diamond with us wherever we went.

Cut to me getting up and carrying my tray a few tables over to stand behind a goth kid with hair dyed black and eyeliner circling his eyes. The camera would pull back to show the whole cafeteria frozen, stone silent. You're thinking, *Oh man, this sporty kid is going to dump his Jell-O all over that other kid's head.* But here's where my life differs from a movie: in real life, I wasn't going over there to bully him. I was going over there to sit down and talk. I was genuinely curious about what made this kid want to come to school in black lipstick. The first time I went over to talk to him, I'm pretty sure he thought I was gonna mess with him, but that wasn't it at all. I was interested in his life, his story. How he made the decisions he did, what made him tick.

The way I see it is that the moment you stop being curious about other people and you begin to let differences stand between you, you start to put them in the category "other." You go from "we" to "not like me." You become self-centered, and when that happens, you start to see other people only in terms of what they can do for you. I feel like every kid wonders at some point if the whole world is just a video game created around them with other people there for the sole purpose of basic interaction. But other people aren't props. That's what gets under my skin about the traditional idea of networking. It's all about making relationships transactional, about "I scratch your back, you scratch mine." When I meet someone, I don't approach them with an agenda of "What can I get out of this person later?" I'm genuinely looking to understand people and learn from them. And that's what has made my network so strong. It's never been about "What can you do for me?" or "How am I going to need you?" It's about getting to know who you are, how you think, what gets you up in the morning, and the ways we're made better together.

Radical connectors know that humanity is like the earth. We have a common core way deep down that's solid, shared, and unchanging. And then we have a uniqueness closer to the surface where we can be as different as a mountain is from the sea. Radical connectors have this incredible binocular vision where they can see both the depths of someone's humanity as well as the differences that sit closer to the surface. The result is that a radical connector can see people as the multidimensional, complicated beings we all are.

Radical connectors are also fearless. They don't pick and choose who gets invited into their circles based on how much they have in common with someone, and that takes guts. Radical connectors are okay muddling through a little awkwardness if the payoff is a richer, more interesting group of people in their lives. They don't go through life skimming for the "right" people to share their time with. They see the merit of an open network. You let people in and you're better for it.

Any farmer will tell you that one of the keys to a successful harvest is to rotate your crops. You switch one crop out for another over different growing seasons. Keep the same crop in place year after year and you deplete the soil of nutrients, ending up with a higher probability of pests and weeds and a paltry crop. Same deal with your diet. If you eat the same thing every single day—even if it's the healthiest salad ever made—you're going to get plenty of one vitamin but not enough of another, and it's going to make you weaker in the long run. Your network is the same. If it's made up of only one type of person, it's going to be weak.

I've wrestled with the fact that people seem to gravitate toward people who look and act and think the same way that they look and act and think. Next time you go to a park, look around. See if you can guess who is with which group. I bet it's surprisingly easy to do so, just based on how people dress, the music they're listening to, the type of gear they've brought with them. We cluster together in clumps of likeness. We live next to people who read and watch and discuss all the same things we read and watch and discuss. Too many of us are *comfortable connectors*, deepening the ruts of our personalities and ideas by hanging out only with people who share them. We need to change tactics and become radical connectors, pollinators who pick up ideas from one spot and carry them to another, cultivating the world we all share. Because here's the thing: it's only when we bump up against something different from ourselves that we either learn something new or have a chance to deepen our beliefs.

I have a favorite history lesson, one that I've shared before. It comes from our sixteenth president, Abraham Lincoln. When you think of Lincoln you might think "beard and stovepipe hat" and "Emancipation Proclamation," but I think "radical connector." When he won the Republican nomination for president in 1860, he beat out New York senator William H. Seward, Ohio governor Salmon P. Chase, and statesman Edward Bates from Missouri.[2] All three of those men were light-years more accomplished than Lincoln, a one-term member of the House of Representatives who had lost not once but *twice* when he'd run for Senate.

As you can imagine, his opponents were less than pleased when this out-of-left-field upstart beat them out for president. However, one of Lincoln's first moves in office showed that he wasn't just some lucky amateur but a once-in-a-lifetime leader. He immediately appointed Seward, Chase, and Bates to his cabinet—a pretty gutsy move that showed both confidence and humility. There was every likelihood that these more established statesmen would be able to outmaneuver Lincoln, wrestling the ship's wheel out of his hands and attempting to steer the country themselves. But Lincoln knew he'd be better off surrounded by people who didn't think exactly as he did, that having his former adversaries nearby would hone his own thinking like a whetstone. The strategy worked out pretty well for Lincoln. Not only is he revered as one of our most beloved presidents but he managed to win the respect of his former rivals by drawing them close and respecting their views.

CAST A TEAM OF RIVALS

Name three people you know you can count on to call you out or consistently challenge you. Before making important decisions, check in with at least one of them to get their candid take.

My personal network contains a lot of devil's advocates. The friction of their opposing views either changes or sharpens my own. Take this book. When I first got the idea, I knew I wanted to do a book about how I've been building a network my whole life, but when I started telling people about it, the response was mixed. Jo got it right away, and so did my parents and a few other people in my inner circle, but our publishers were less enthusiastic. They thought the world already had enough books about networking and they hinted (strongly) that I should pivot and come up with another topic. That feedback was a thousand times more motivating and useful to me than the soundest pat on the back would have been. If they weren't getting it, I knew I needed to refine my idea, dig deeper, and clarify my intention. Without their extremely polite but very firm resistance, my idea would have been less focused.

I can see how it might be instinctive to stick with people whose motivations and ideals align perfectly with your own. But a dynamic network will never be built on likeness. Think about it: if I were to populate my life with people who talk, act, and think just like me, my network would be completely one-dimensional, lopsided. And if you've ever built anything, you know how lopsided foundations turn out. Without fresh vantage points and opposing ideas, there's no opportunity to be strengthened. No change. No growth. No new ideas.

A dynamic network will never be built on likeness. #makesense

We have to be willing to engage with people who are different from us and do so with dignity and love. The Trappist monk Thomas Merton wrote, "The beginning of love is to let those we love be perfectly themselves and not to twist them to fit our own image. Otherwise we love only the reflection of ourselves we find in them."[3] Man, that rings true. If we are going to lead with love, we have to love our fellow man in the fullness of who they are, not just the parts that remind us of ourselves.

Recent societal events have made this even clearer. I can't remember a period during my lifetime when the world has seemed more divided. We as a nation have been hurt, and as a result we've let negative emotions lead the way: fear, judgment, and hate. That's the lie we've somehow perpetuated—that disagreement must be met with vitriol or anger. Instead of hurling insults, try to play the role of a radical connector. Set aside your need to be right and aim for understanding instead. When you are at odds, ask yourself where the other person is coming from. Trust that they formed their ideas in the cauldron of experience and inheritance just like you have.

I recently saw a video made by a man named Emmanuel Acho called "Uncomfortable Conversations with a Black Man." This was shortly after George Floyd's death had sparked a series of protests across the nation and caused a lot of people to do some much-needed reckoning. Acho had made the video in response to the dozens of questions he'd gotten from his white friends about his experience as a Black man. In the video he spoke candidly about how our country needs to change course because if we don't, we are headed for a collision. He explained how the pain of not feeling like he belonged had shaped his whole life. He talked about how living unconsciously is a privilege. He didn't deny that white people have pain, because of course we do; he just pointed out that our pain doesn't come from the color of our skin.[4]

A light bulb went on as I listened to him talk. I thought, *I've been blind to this reality my whole life*. That is not an easy thing to admit. I grew up in Texas in the '70s, a time and place where it wasn't uncommon to hear words dropped in casual conversation that would rightly bring a room to a halt today. I've tried to be fair and to treat people with respect and to teach my children to do the same, but maybe I wasn't going far enough. Once I saw it, I couldn't unsee it. It hit me that I didn't even know half the stuff that Black people are struggling with. My eyes were being opened to scenarios that I didn't even know existed, whether it was being watched carefully while you were just trying to buy some new shoes or living with the knowledge that laws are systemically inequitable and inconsistently applied. Acho said that he had to calculate every move he made whenever he left his house so that his actions wouldn't be misinterpreted as threats.[5]

The name of those videos is right on the money—they are uncomfortable. But growth always is.

My thinking shifted that day. I was reminded that it's every bit as important to understand how different someone's experience might be from yours and how it shaped them as it is to take comfort in the knowledge of all we have in common.

An open, pliable mind is the starting point for radical connection, but we need to do more than pay attention. Paying attention is good, but we're not just making a book report by gathering data on our fellow humans. We need to let what we learn from paying attention activate a sense of empathy and foster connection.

The next step is action. Lucky for us, we've been given a custom-made tool to foster understanding—the ability to talk. No, I'm not being a smart aleck. I'm serious. Language is an incredible gift. A little wind going over our vocal cords and a little something in our ears vibrating let us exchange ideas with other people and help us get inside their heads and understand them. We've been given language as a way to thread ourselves together. We have to use it. You might screw it up a couple of times. People might even think you're a bumbling idiot on occasion. Sometimes, you're going to strike out. But if the payoff is more connection, more compassion, more understanding, I'll take looking like a fool any day of the week. That's the currency we should be offering one another—vulnerability and understanding—not "What can you do for me?" and quid pro quo.

That's it.

That's my big advice.

Talk to other people, those who are just like you as well as those who aren't. As you choose people for your network, look for radical connectors—people who do the same. Seek out people who show genuine interest in one another, who can both see our common core and celebrate what makes us unique.

I'm aware that someone could read this and think, *Easy for you to say, Gaines. You just told us at the beginning of this chapter that you were born a people person.* My telling you to get out there and radically connect might come off like a guy who has written a fitness book saying, "My secret? Well, I have always been incredible at eating properly and working out. Now excuse me as I polish off this green juice and run this forty-yard dash in four seconds flat." I get it. You might not have come out of the womb wanting to talk to people. Maybe you're shy and you can't fathom speaking to a stranger. I don't have the fear factor when it comes to talking to people, but I know plenty of people who do. Heck, I'm married to one. Trust me: you are far from alone.

As a matter of fact, I was listening to an interview the other day with the Pulitzer Prize–winning reporter Wesley Lowery. He confessed something to the interviewer: he hated approaching people. A reporter! It was *his job* to approach strangers—a job he's obviously very good at, because they don't give Pulitzers to just any hack. And even though he had a very legitimate reason to talk to people, he avoided doing it. What was really interesting to me was the way he handled making a connection: he asked a small, simple question, which led to another, and another, and before long, he'd find himself engaged in a meaningful dialogue.[6] Asking a question is like a key moving the gears in a complicated lock. Each turn gets you closer to unlocking the treasure hidden within that person.

Give it a try. When you have a chance to make a connection, start by thinking of something that you might want to know about that person. Maybe you're at a café and you notice a dad whose kid is wearing a soccer jersey, so you wonder if your kid has played against their team. Maybe you notice that the barista has got a drop of paint on their shoes and you wonder if it came from a wall or a canvas. Maybe the person in front of you is a regular who always orders six coffees to go and you wonder who the other five are for. The first step toward radical connection is taking the time to get interested.

If you can work up the nerve, go further. Ask your question. Then listen to the answer and see if they don't ask you one in return. Pass the thread back and forth between you until you are tied together. Once you make that connection, that moment of human joining, let it hold you. But someone has to make the first move. Someone has to start the process, and I'm more than happy for that someone to be me.

BOTTOM LINE

Learn to let people in.
You'll be better for it.

CHAPTER 10

INTERACTIONS, NOT TRANSACTIONS

Listen, it takes an awful lot to scare me. I don't bat an eyelash when I imagine myself in a position where I'd have to go to extremes to protect my family. If they needed me to, I would absolutely run into a burning building or jump on a bomb that is about to go off. Every time. Lay that on me, and don't worry about it. I'm built for complicated, hard stuff. But in the past couple years, I've had one or two experiences that have flat out scared the hell out of me.

Before I go on, I want to say that I know this chapter could very well blow up in my face. There's a chance you're going to read this and go, "Cry me a river. Come talk to me when you've got real problems." But I wear my heart and my personality right on my sleeve, and I'm telling you about this because I believe it matters. I'm asking you to keep your arrows in the quiver for just a moment and hear me out.

Here goes.

A few times a year, Jo and I rent a U-Haul, pack up the kids, and head out to this enormous outdoor flea market called Round Top. You might have seen it on some episodes of *Fixer Upper.* Thousands of people come from all over the world to the fairgrounds in this one-square-mile town to hunt through eight million pieces of vintage whatever. You want to find a white wicker daybed, you're in luck. If you need a set of antlers from an eight-point buck, they have that. Always wanted a sign from an old pencil factory? You've come to the right place. Round Top gives off this great festival-like atmosphere where your heart beats a little faster with possibility.

When we go, Jo and I get a kick out of watching the kids hunting around for treasure. Round Top is great for discovering old things and bringing them new life, and it's always been a really special place to us.

We headed out there one afternoon a couple years into *Fixer Upper.* We were making our way through tables covered in all kinds of wares when, about an hour in, Duke tugged on my shirt to tell me about some little thing that had caught his eye a few vendors back—an old toy or some baseball cards or who knows what. I told Jo, "I'm gonna take Duke back there a second. We'll catch up with you later." Duke and I walked off hand in hand.

We had gone just a couple of yards when some people recognized me from the show and started gathering 'round, wanting to talk. Just a few people at first, but then a few more, and before long a real crowd had formed. I appreciate when folks take the time to tell me and Jo what our show has meant to them. To hear that we brightened someone's day or somehow inspired them means a lot to me, and I hate to let people down when they've gone out of their way to say something nice, so I stopped to talk.

As I got through about my third conversation, I realized I hadn't seen Duke in a minute. Now, I'm not the kind of parent who's always looking for my kid to get abducted. We live out in the country, so it's not uncommon for the kids to wander off for an afternoon. I'm more the type to say, "Go on, ride your bike on down to the creek to look for minnows. Just be back by dark." So it wasn't alarming that he got away from me, but it was a big crowd and the boy was only seven. I told the people around me, "You all, hold on one second, please. I need to find my son. Has anybody seen him? Seven years old, about yay big?"

I'd barely gotten the words out when this woman took me by the arm and started leading me in another direction. I was relieved someone was willing to help me look for Duke, but then she started saying something about how her mother would just love to have a picture with me. I'm sure this woman was a decent person, and I'm sure her mother was very nice, but my *kid* was missing, and it was like she didn't hear that at all. She didn't see me as a concerned father. She saw the goofy guy she felt like she knew from TV and thought it would be a hoot to have a picture with him.

I finally spotted Duke over by the entrance to a big white tent. I pulled myself away and took off toward him, and when I reached him, he went, "Dad, it's okay. I'm right here." No big deal. Everybody was fine. Of course. Nobody nabbed him. He hadn't disappeared in the sea of people. Nothing had happened.

Except it had.

Like I said, in a lot of ways I'm a tough guy. You likely picture me grinning like an idiot as I bust through a wall, and it's true that it doesn't bother me much when a piece of two-by-four hits me square in the shoulder. But the fact is, there's something I feel at a real deep level. I'm absolutely terrified of letting someone down. Jo isn't that way. When it comes to her kids, she would've plowed through that crowd without a second thought. But that afternoon at Round Top there was a part of me that felt like I needed to give those people what they wanted.

Doing so came at a cost. Even though I was the center of attention, I could tell that no one in the crowd had seen *me*. They saw an idea of me, an impression. They hadn't been thinking about my fears or the fact that I was there with my kid and maybe I might prefer to enjoy some shopping and eat a corndog rather than do an impromptu meet-and-greet. I wasn't a person to them in that moment; I was a commodity. An easy mark to get a few more likes on social media.

It's like we haven't learned how to see beyond ourselves. I've been guilty of this myself. A few years back, Jo and I were at the airport when I spotted Rangers legend Nolan Ryan waiting to board his own flight not but a few hundred feet away from us. I'm telling you, the time in between me recognizing who he was and introducing myself couldn't have been more than ten seconds. I didn't even think about the situation beyond the fact that this was *Nolan freakin' Ryan.* The Ryan Express himself, in the flesh. He was kind about it; he shook my hand and introduced his wife. It all went down in less than a minute. But as I turned back toward Jo, other people nearby had started to recognize who he was now that I'd gone and made a big deal of it, and a small crowd started to form around him. I was starting to realize how selfish it was of me to interrupt his sweet time with his wife like that. And for what? Because I was able to spot him in a crowd? That somehow earned me the opportunity to be known by him? I walked away thinking, *I can't believe I made that all about me.*

Strange as it sounds, up until that day at Round Top, things like anxiety and depression and hopelessness weren't familiar feelings to me. But something about that interaction just knocked me over. Who I was had gotten obscured by the *image* of who I was. I had these overwhelming feelings of hopelessness. That moment of missed human connection punched me right in the gut. I never want to make another person feel that way—like they've been completely dehumanized, cut from the network of humanity.

When Jo and I agreed to do *Fixer Upper* the first time around, we weren't in "the industry." We certainly weren't TV people. Heck, we'd never been on a set. We didn't know anything about producers or microphones or camera equipment. We certainly did not know one single thing about fame. We were just not prepared for the intensity of the situation we ended up in.

It felt like our lives changed overnight. We went from being two people with a couple of reasonably successful small businesses to people who constantly had to tell friends of ours, "I know what it said in the tabloids, but Jo and I are not getting divorced / having twins / relocating to Los Angeles."

Jo and I had been saying to each other, *This is going to be okay when things go back to normal.* But months passed and normal was nowhere to be seen. We started to think, *Wait, what if it never goes back to normal?* It was strangling the life out of me. I couldn't breathe, and when I went to work, which I should have been excited about, I had anxiety instead. The more people saw me as Chip Gaines, Celebrity, the less I felt like Chip Gaines, the person.

My natural desire to connect with people short-circuited because those connections started to feel more like transactions. It sent me scurrying into a shell like a recluse, which is absolutely *not* my nature. Suddenly it felt like I had a split personality. Sometimes, I'm the me I've known all my life: curious, eager, ready to talk to anyone. Then there's this other guy who is kind of wary, not so outgoing.

It causes major cognitive dissonance to find myself shying away from people instead of leaning in toward them, because that completely contradicts who I am. I *love* people. So then why are there times when I find myself walking into a room with my eyes locked straight ahead so I don't accidentally make eye contact with anyone and give them a reason to talk to me? I start to justify my behavior, thinking, *I don't have time for this* or *I'm doing him a favor; I'm feeling so cagey, he wouldn't want to talk to me anyway.* The real problem is that I actually started to believe I was better off not reaching out, not risking a connection.

They say you don't fully appreciate the importance of what you had until it's gone. What I have found in my moments of reclusiveness is a certainty that we can do better in how we see one another. We can widen our lenses. We can remind ourselves that people are so much more than who they are in relation to us.

I've never been a royal watcher, but I've paid attention to Meghan Markle after her marriage to Prince Harry. Her candor about what it's been like to be thrust into the spotlight got me.

She's been interviewed a thousand times, and you've got to appreciate her honesty. She did one interview for the documentary *Harry & Meghan* where she went *deep*. She talked about how hard it was to be under a microscope when she was a newlywed and a new mom, a time when you are at your most vulnerable. At one point the interviewer, Tom Bradby, asked her about the impact the pressure she is under has had on her mental health. Basically, all the guy said was, "I know this has to be tough. How are you doing?" and Meghan was so moved by the question that she almost burst into tears. She thanked him for asking because not many people had thought to ask if she was okay. You could palpably feel that small act of compassion cracking her shell. It obviously meant the world to her to be seen as a fellow human instead of as a scoop. To watch this strong, dynamic woman struggling with this was nothing short of heartbreaking.[1]

I could see how someone might watch that video and go, "Please. I can't make my mortgage payment. You're stinking gorgeous. You were a successful actress. You married a prince, and you got to move into a castle—which part of that is supposed to make me feel sorry for you?"

A shiny golden cage is still a cage.

You see why I'm worried I'm going to lose you: because I'm talking about fame—but it just happens that fame is the lens that has flattened me in other people's eyes. But famous people are not the only ones who get flattened. Far from it. And that's why this is so important.

To flatten someone is to crush them, extracting only what is useful to you and ignoring the rest. No surprise, that feels just awful.

A dear friend of mine from college named Jason has a son, Matthew, whose friends call him Matty, who was born with cystic fibrosis. If you want to see what it means to love with your whole heart, you've got to meet Jason. He is completely devoted to this kid.

I called Jason the other day. We talked about this and that, and then I asked after Matthew. When Jason responded, something weird happened with his voice. It got real tight, like someone was squeezing at his throat while he spoke, and he started rattling off test results and medical terms.

After a few seconds he caught himself and said, "Chip, man, I'm sorry. I went into automatic update mode. I forgot I was talking to a real friend for a minute there." Then he said something interesting. He said that he'd found that there are two types of people who ask about Matthew's health. The first kind are people who really do care, who see Matthew not just as a walking illness but who can see that it's a double heartbreak that the kid can't even do the same types of things the other kids can do. Then there's the second kind—people who ask questions and make it clear that what they're looking for is an executive summary of Matthew's condition. Just the facts, preferably new ones. They want information they can own and ration out as they see fit at a PTA meeting or their bridge club, shaking their heads in a big show of sympathy and saying, "Did you hear the latest about Matthew? His results are in and, well, it's not good. Such a shame. Such a nice family."

What really struck me was that Jason said that the lion's share of people are in the curious camp, not the compassionate camp, and as a result, he has started to go into every situation with his gloves up. And by the way, when I say curious, I don't mean genuinely interested. I mean self-servingly nosy. Think how lonely that must be for this family. When they could be supported by a web of connection, instead they find themselves feeling isolated.

Flattening isn't always quite that blatant. Many things can flatten a three-dimensional person into a two-dimensional state. It could be that people see only what you can do for them, their experience of you in the past, stereotypes they have about you, or what they have heard about you from someone else. But that is just not enough information for them to know the full you.

Taffy Brodesser-Akner, a journalist who has written a piece about Jo and me along with some of the most memorable profiles ever for places like the *New York Times* and *GQ*, told an interviewer that even when the subject liked a piece she'd written about them, they were usually disappointed by it because it didn't show the full picture.[2] Of course that's true. You can't compress a life into a couple thousand words. And you can't compress a person into what you know about them or what they mean to you. Any conclusion you draw based on a handful of data points will be, at best, only half the equation.

I bet you've felt flattened at one time or another. Maybe someone didn't listen to you, or they made an assumption, or they treated you as a means to an end. Maybe someone held back information they didn't think you could handle. Or you were stereotyped because of your religion or political affiliation. How did that feel? We need to widen our view of one another in order to take in the whole picture.

Flattening happens to dentists, teachers, plumbers, carpenters, mechanics, editors, therapists, electricians, interior decorators, landscapers—just about anyone. I think about my doctor. The woman can't go out to breakfast without someone coming over to her table to say, "I'm so sorry. I see you're enjoying your pancakes, but I've been trying to get ahold of your office, and your secretary says you've been on vacation. I've had the worst rash on my leg. It's itchy and red, and well, here, would you mind taking a look for yourself?"

When you adjust your lens so that you can see all of someone, not just the role they fill for you, it's like a character in a play walked off the stage and into your life. While they are up there on the stage, you have a one-way connection where you passively take, take, take. But when they come down, suddenly you're rocking and rolling, asking questions, getting to see everything from a million new angles. It's a game changer for both of you. The role stops being scripted and expected. You open yourself up to surprise and discovery, and the payoff for both of you is huge.

We need to widen our view of one another in order to take in the whole picture. #makesense

How do you think of the people in your life? As *your* doctor? *Your* babysitter? *Your* plumber? Absolutely. But that is only who they are in relation to you. I'll bet they don't think of themselves exclusively as that one thing—as just a boss or a mom or a terrific cook. They have a kaleidoscope of other interests, constantly shifting and calling their attention. Me, I'm a husband, a father, an entrepreneur, a son, an animal lover, a business owner, a goofball, a baseball fan, and about three hundred other things all at once. It's not any one of those parts that defines me; it's how they work together. I bring all of them with me into the world, and the same is true of you. The people you want in your network are the people who see you as more than a LinkedIn connection.

Imagine how that moment at Round Top could have gone if the people I'd been talking to had seen beyond what I could do for them to the concerned dad I was. If only someone in that crowd had just said, "Let's take a breath. What was your son wearing?" They would have really touched my life, we would have shared a moment of real human connection, and we would have been linked together in a very sincere and authentic way.

The point is life is too short to miss out on one another.

BOTTOM LINE

When in doubt .. Go with the
— Golden Rule —

CHAPTER 11

ENGAGE OR ELSE

A few years ago one of our employees at Magnolia had a sign made for my office with this quote from comedian Tommy Smothers: "When you don't know what you're talking about, it's hard to know when you're finished." I laughed it off because, while it wasn't entirely a compliment, it was entirely true. It's typical for me to turn basically anything meant to be a "quick touchpoint" at the office into several hours of conversation.

Maybe you're thinking, *Man, that guy must love the sound of his own voice.* But I promise you, that's not it at all. I mean it when I say that I genuinely love to engage with people. I always have. That moment of exchange between one human and another—that's the stuff I live for. That connection that comes with being fully present with someone. And if it's you I'm talking to, you better believe you've got my full attention. I am actually pretty particular about tuning out any potential distractions in those moments. So much so that it's become common for me to get caught up in a conversation with someone at the office or a job site, or a complete stranger at the hardware store. We'll be in the middle of something and I lose all track of time. It's *bad*. I've got a track record of being late to meet Jo that runs all the way back to our first date.

In my twenties, this was usually no big deal. The stakes weren't too high if I was late to meet a friend or started work a little late, 'cause I could always make it up the second half of the day. But once Jo and I were married and our family started to grow, all of a sudden being late to pick up Drake, our firstborn, from practice because I wanted to hammer out one last detail with an employee resulted in poor Drakey feeling like his dad had forgotten him. Pulling up to the house well past dinnertime because someone I'd passed on the road needed help changing a tire left me feeling like I'd chosen a stranger over my own family.

Those feelings took me a while to wrap my mind around. I'd always believed that stopping to help someone on the side of the road was the decent thing. And that staying late at the office to help a team member get a project across the finish line is what any good boss would do. More than that, I'd always believed that my instinct to engage with someone was a way of holding me accountable to my character and the things I value. If I say I care about authentic connection, then I want to genuinely care about authentic connection.

So what was with that queasy feeling in my stomach?

I knew the answer. Now that we had a family, the weight of things had shifted. My heart for connection was, at times, shrouding my responsibility to my family. Being fully present with someone else was occasionally costing me time with my wife, with my kids.

Now, I never want my kids to see me pass by someone in need without so much as pulling over to ask if they could use a little help. That's real important to me. But the reality is, when you do choose to stop to lend someone a hand, or you choose to let that conversation keep rolling, whoever or whatever was waiting for you is going to be disappointed.

You've taken time away from them or you've missed out on a moment you can't get back.

Because it is, and always will be, physically impossible to be in two places at once, I've had to learn the hard way how to balance that part of me who desires to engage well while also being fully present for the very people that make up the best parts of me.

The way I see it, we each have a satchel that's filled with what makes us who we are. It's a bag we carry with us everywhere we go. But it's only so big.

When you're packing it up, you want to put in the most important things first—your relationships, your family, your spouse, your calling, your faith, your health, your values. The things that, if you lost them, would leave your life truly empty. If you fill that satchel up with rinky-dink stuff that gets tossed in there on a whim, you're not going to be able to fit the things you really need in the limited space that's left—which is why you have to *choose* to put the important stuff in first. Not the easy stuff, or the stuff calling loudest for your attention, or the stuff that will make you look best, but the stuff that gives your life meaning.

For me, life begins and ends with me loving Jo with all my heart. Same deal goes for my kids. I will be their very best dad always. Then there's my faith, without which the other two wouldn't be possible. That's already a pretty full bag, but it's a load I can carry upright.

But if there comes a time when the contents of the bag change—whether something falls out without my noticing, or I need to make room for something else, or things get even *slightly* off balance—my whole world turns on its axis. That is exactly what happened when Jo and I started a family.

Before we had kids, I filled my life by loving on Jo and loving my work so much that I wanted every day of the week to be a workday, because it didn't even feel like work to me. It felt as natural and life-sustaining as breathing.

Then the contents of the bag changed. I started to realize that too much time dedicated to my work was going to mean missing out on time with our babies. I felt lopsided, and I knew that the original balance wasn't going to work for me anymore. A new nonnegotiable was at play, and it wasn't hard for me to see that I needed to recalibrate. I shifted things around so that I could be there when it counted.

But I want to tell you about a time recently when I was so out of whack that I nearly toppled over.

At forty-five I'm not the young stud I used to be. I've got a few extra pounds, and I've traded my position as a badass on the field for one as a dad cheering nervously from the bleachers. Fact of the matter is, I am smack dab in the demographic for a midlife crisis. If you're looking for me to sneak out on Jo, tear across the country on a Harley, and wake up in a hotel room with no memory of how on earth I got there, you're gonna be disappointed. But I do have to be real with you.

I shared in chapter 10 about the season of my life when I got knocked sideways by the feeling that my connections had become more like transactions. That lasted a while. I'd always been resilient, so I was thrown off when this disconnected feeling seemed like it was fixing to park itself inside me for good. I started to grapple with some pretty big stuff—I'm talking meaning-of-life, what's-it-all-about, is-this-all-there-is questions. Maybe that's not what you came for, but I promise this whole chapter isn't all doom and gloom, so hold on a minute.

I once asked my dad if he'd ever had a midlife crisis. He shook his head and said, "Midlife crisis? Absolutely not. I never had one of those. I never ran off with my secretary or bought a Corvette with my retirement savings."

I told him, "No, Dad, that's not what I meant. I wasn't trying to catch you in some sort of trap with that question. I meant, did you ever worry that you'd wasted your life? Did you ever question your identity? That sort of crisis."

He just snorted and said, "Oh that? Everybody has one of those."

Knowing I wasn't the only one didn't make me feel all that much better. I'd only ever been confident about who I was and where I was heading, but to be really frank, the last two or three years it was like someone had turned down the volume on all of my senses. Things that used to excite me no longer did. I even started to avoid some of them, mostly stuff that involved other people, which, for a guy who thinks of himself as a people person, was a knee-buckling reality. I'm usually a fun-loving guy, but I wasn't feeling very fun. I didn't want to let anyone down by being a bummer, so I tried to act like my old self even though I didn't feel like my old self. I'd crack jokes so people would laugh, and I'd start telling old stories to people when it was obvious that was what they'd been hoping to hear. But there were a lot of days when that would just make me feel like I was a phony, which was even worse. I got skittish about putting myself in positions where there would be pressure to act happier than I felt, so I became pretty antisocial. But the consequence of that was that I cut off my fuel supply, the charge I get from other people that has kept me going most of my life.

Each morning I woke up and it was Groundhog Day. Every day felt like the day before. Everywhere I went it felt like I was having the same conversation that I'd already had one thousand times with one thousand different people. It was never unique. It was never interesting. It was never different. It was never authentic. It was freakin' awful.

Occasionally, I'd get a flicker, the picture would tune in, and a glimmer of my old self would come into focus. On those days, Jo would say, "Chip, you seem like you're good. Are you good?" And sometimes I was. But mostly, I wasn't good. I was just acting how I thought Chip Gaines should act. I'd lost something important to me, one of the major parts of my identity that I usually held close. I was radically off balance.

What you value has the potential to hurt you, and I was hurting. If you lose a trinket, it's no big thing. You go right on with your life. But if you lose something that matters to you, or if you never managed to get your hands on something like that in the first place, you've got a hole that leaves a painful wound.

We feel pain for a reason. It is a signal telling us that something's not right, and it can stop us short. It can happen with all the force of a riptide. You're swimming along okay, and suddenly something starts pulling you out and forces you to let go of whatever you've got so you don't end up floating out to sea. You let go of what you have in your arms so you can swim back to shore. But then that thing is gone, and you're sitting there utterly crushed with nothing but shame at failing to hold on to it tighter. There's also a whole lot of anxiety that you'll never get back what you lost.

You know how I said at the beginning of this book that you don't choose books; they choose you? Well, during this season, Viktor Frankl's book *Man's Search for Meaning* came into my life. A business acquaintance of mine had passed it to me a while back. I didn't know a thing about it, and honestly, it didn't grab me immediately. It seemed way too scientific, and the guy on the back cover looked like he was about one hundred years old. I started pecking at the first chapter, which begins with Frankl in a concentration camp. We're talking heavy, the worst of the worst of humanity. It was far from a light read. I'd get through a couple of paragraphs and then I'd have to close the book and regroup. I couldn't really settle into a groove with it.

Heading out on vacation last summer, we were running late and in a big hurry to get to the plane, so I asked Jo to grab my book from our bedroom. I thought she knew which one I meant—a business book I had on my nightstand. It was one of those stories about how a big-deal guy made his way to the top. I got on the plane, all excited to read an inspiring up-by-the-bootstraps story. Instead I reached into my backpack and pulled out this book about surviving in a concentration camp. Not quite what I was planning. But there I was on the flight with some time to kill, so I figured I might as well give it another try. I picked up on page 10 where I'd left off, and the most amazing thing happened. By the time we landed a couple of hours later, I was nearly done with it. I couldn't put it down.

If you've read the book, you know that Frankl pivots midway through to introduce his philosophy of logotherapy—healing the soul through finding meaning in life. That's when it started to feel like he was basically calling me by name. His message went straight to my heart.

He was talking about the psychological struggle we all face and the potholes we encounter in our lives, the ones that threaten to swallow us whole if we let them. But he was very clear: we don't have to let them. No matter what circumstances we find ourselves in—and he was in the worst imaginable—we can choose our attitude. I'm telling you, this book should be required reading for every single person on the planet. I underlined and made more notes in it than any book I've ever read. He put into words so many ideas I had been wrestling with.

I kept reading passages aloud to anyone who would listen. My poor kids would be walking through the room on their way to the pool, and I'd grab them and say, "Come here. You've got to hear this." They'd hang for a moment and then be like, "Okay, Dad, thanks for the lesson on the meaning of life. [Pause.] Can we go swim now?"

Long story longer, Frankl insists that the freedom to choose how you spend your life rests within you. He warns against becoming "a plaything of circumstance."[1] That's what happens when you aren't deliberate about what you put in your satchel. A bunch of stuff you don't need fills it up. The part we tend to forget is that it's *your* satchel. You get to decide what to put in there. You get to decide every day what you will do, the attitude you have toward your circumstances, and how to spend your days. The thing is, you've got to act.

Let's say you love to paint, always have. You can think of yourself as an artist all you want, but if you never make time to sit your canvas down by a picturesque landscape or a nice bowl of fruit because you spend your days helping people fill out their tax forms, I hate to break it to you, but you're an accountant. Maybe you don't need to quit your job as an accountant to devote yourself to being a starving artist, but you do need to pick up a paintbrush once in a while.

In the same way, I have always believed myself to be someone who loves people, but I wasn't acting like one. Action counts, and action takes effort and intention.

I looked up the word "intention" and found that it comes from the Latin *intentionem*, meaning "a stretching out, straining, exertion, effort."[2] Look at those words. There's not a passive thing about them. Engaging with your life and acting deliberately isn't necessarily easy. There are so many forces out there pushing against you; it's real work to act with intention. But the stakes are too high not to.

I took some time to reflect. I'd been treating other people like they were unwelcome interruptions, something to be avoided. Slowly, I started to realize that moment in Round Top was the tipping point that initiated this whole thing. For the first time in my life, my relationships were right there in front of me and I'd been ignoring them like they were getting in the way of something else I had to do. Except people are not interruptions to your life. They are life.

That's what I was missing when I was struggling with my identity: the connections to people in my network who held me. I'd spent my whole life building a network, but now I wasn't relying on it. I don't know what made me so gun-shy about turning to my people for help. After all, we are built to take care of one another when we're in need. It's part of what makes us human.

Being connected nourishes us. We are a social species, made to be with one another, to work together, to join our lives. And yet, I read about a study that showed that more than half of American adults would describe themselves as lonely.[3] Let that sink in for a minute. Even if you set aside how sad that is, you can look at how loneliness affects our health to see how important it is for us to connect.

There are so many forces out there pushing against you; it's real work to act with intention. But the stakes are too high not to. #makesense

According to a neuroscientist known as Dr. Loneliness, our bodies react to being socially isolated as an emergency.[4] Feeling alone activates the very same part of our brains as the fear center that lights up when we encounter a threat to our physical health, like encountering a swarm of bees or standing too close to the edge of a cliff. It's that serious. Our lives literally depend on our ability to connect.

I'd been talking to Jo all along about what was bothering me, and we came to the conclusion together that it was our network of people that was missing. I'd retreated to the company of Jo and the kids when I'd felt on edge around other people. And as a result our marriage was as good as it had ever been. But one of the ramifications was it was putting a lot of pressure on Jo and the kids to be everything I needed. I realized that I'd let the pendulum swing too far. I'd drifted away from my other relationships. And I found out that my network is only as a strong as all of its parts.

My network was there for me to reach out to, draw on for strength, and to remind me that connection is as life-sustaining as the breath in our lungs. We humans are meant to connect; our hearts are naturally drawn toward one another.

It was a little painful, like warmth coming back into frostbitten fingers. The people in my network might have been the ones listening, but I heard something in their willingness to do so, something I had needed to hear for a long time. Someone had cleared the fuzz out of my ears and a voice was whispering, "It's time for you to show back up."

I'd thought being gregarious and the life of the party was the only way people were going to like me. Those qualities are still a part of me, and I'm glad folks appreciate that I can be a goofball. But when I realized that I could choose to be that way only when it felt normal and authentic and real, and at *no other time*, I felt a thousand pounds lighter. No longer did I need to "perform" when someone told me to act that way, or when I sensed that's how someone expected me to act, and not when I acted that way by default.

Irony of ironies, the more grounded by authentic connections I became, the lighter I felt. I came out of the fog and began to engage. Sensors on, I was locked and loaded, ready for life and all it has to offer.

Life is full of surprises when you choose to really engage. There's a quote I love that crystallizes this mindset for me: "There are only two ways to live your life. One is as though nothing is a miracle. The other is as though everything is a miracle." If you're in the nothing's-a-miracle camp, there's no point in searching for miracles because you've already concluded that they don't exist. But I say there's nothing boring about this miraculous world around us unless we let ourselves become numb to it. It's like we say in our Magnolia Manifesto: "Today is a gift and everyday miracles are scattered about if only we have eyes to see."

And for me, there's no greater miracle than a sincere and authentic bond between people.

The thing about this miraculous feeling of being connected and engaged is that it's already there, always available for the taking. You just need to do a little mental weed-whacking to clear out the junk that is keeping you from seeing with clear eyes. Because when you cut the distracting clutter out of your life, you'll find there's a deep contentment that comes from being able to engage deliberately instead of playing Whac-A-Mole with less important things. You can find it sitting on a couple of lawn chairs and having a talk with a friend, or by yourself in the quiet when you wake up before dawn. Nothing gives me that feeling like being with Jo and the kids. When I'm with them, I'm not worried about how I'm coming off. They don't care what shirt I'm wearing, or expect me to entertain them, or ask me to be anyone other than who I am. There's nothing fancy about the time we spend together as a family. It's not about what money can buy. It's about breakfast and walking around in our PJs and messy hair. It's not about getting on a plane and going to some exotic place or having a once-in-a-lifetime experience; it's about choosing a lifetime full of experiences.

FIND THE UPSIDE OF GETTING KNOCKED DOWN

Make a list—right here, right now—of the hardest things you've gone through in your life. List what came of it, but concentrate on what you learned, how you found a strength you didn't know you had in you.

Difficult Experience	What I Learned / How I Grew

While the going gets tough, consider this list proof that you can come out of it stronger than before.

Now that I'm through what I hope is the worst part, it's not that I'm glad I had what felt to me like an identity crisis. But I am grateful. Hard times forge you. You get to the far side of a difficult time and when you look back on that struggle, it makes you appreciate where you landed. It didn't come easily. It didn't fall out of the sky. Instead you got up and gave your pain purpose.

I've started to think the feeling of disconnection I'd grappled with was in fact what God needed me to have gone through. Why? Maybe so that in this next season I would appreciate what I have all the more. They say hunger is the best sauce, and strange as it sounds, I appreciate my connections even more deeply now after having gone a while without them.

We're now right back to where we started this book, with connection. That's what pulled me from the brink: connecting again with other people.

Think about how powerful it was the last time you could tell that another person was with you, paying close attention to what you were saying, looking you in the eye, not messing around with their phone or thinking about what they're going to do next. They were really with you, not just in the same room, but there with you emotionally. When you have that experience, it's like someone is shining a spotlight on your soul. Let's do *that*. Let's practice lighting each other up. Let's do it by really paying attention. By engaging. Not just for others, but for ourselves.

You can't connect with people if your mind isn't engaged. We've all been to lunch with that friend who is scrolling through Twitter when we're trying to talk about something serious. But what is more engaging, more complicated, more hilarious and confounding than another human being who is right there with us? We owe it to ourselves and to each other to engage and be present for the people in our network. But that means making space in our lives to do so.

Being genuinely present is a kind of caretaking. Presence—real, genuine, uninterrupted presence—is one of the most valuable gifts we can offer another person. Giving your full attention to someone, totally unfiltered, can transform a forgettable moment into something you'll never forget. That's the "tend" part of "attend." If I attend to you, I help you flourish and grow. And vice versa. This is what I mean by an everyday miracle.

My best, most engaged moments are the ones I've chosen. I'm in dirt, doing some chore or another on the farm, nothing between me and the earth but my jeans and my boots. Or I'm trading stories with an old college buddy. Or walking in the evening with Jo as the fireflies light up the sky around us. I've found that life looks pretty dang good when you simply engage.

BOTTOM LINE

Choose to engage & watch your life snap into focus so you can see it clearly for the miracle it is.

CHAPTER 12

LET 'EM GROW

When you submit your senior picture for the yearbook at Grapevine High School in north Texas, you don't have to go to a studio and have a photographer snap a shot of you against a boring, solid-color background. You get to put a little flavor in it. If you're an athlete, you've probably got your letterman jacket on and you're holding your basketball or you're in your Speedo with goggles. If you're in the band, maybe you're holding your tuba or saxophone or what have you.

When it was time to take my picture, I wore my letterman jacket and pulled up in the black Jeep I'd bought when I turned sixteen. To this day I look at that photo and think, "Dang, we sure look good."

I loved that Jeep and drove it everywhere—to school, to baseball practice, heck, if anyone needed a chore done, I was the first one with my hand up to go to the post office or the pharmacy or the hardware store. Anything for another chance to get behind the wheel.

It looked good, but, mechanically speaking, let's just say it left something to be desired—like reliability. I'd be heading home from school, or on the way to pick up a date, and there'd be some terrible noise coming from the rear, or the brakes would scream bloody murder, or the darn thing would just up and quit. Next thing you know, I'm hitchhiking down the interstate trying to get to wherever in the world I was going. But I always managed to MacGyver that baby back into shape and get it back on the road with a few turns of a wrench, some duct tape, and a little bit of luck.

Then, one day during my senior year, I was on my way to baseball practice when all of a sudden smoke started pouring out of the engine. *Dang it, now what? Maybe if I ease up on the gas a little, take the hills gently, it will work itself out.* But nope. The further I drove the more smoke came out. But I couldn't be late to practice, and besides, if I pulled over, who knew if I'd be able to get that Jeep to start again. So, like an idiot, I drove a few miles with smoke billowing out from under the hood.

As soon as I got to the practice field the whole team gathered around me. We propped the hood up and flames literally *jumped* out of the vehicle. Everybody was looking at me like, "Oh crap. Chip's about to get blown up." Thinking fast, I ran over to grab a five-gallon bucket full of practice balls. I dumped them out, and they rolled all over the ground as I raced to the equipment shed and filled up the bucket from a hose. I hauled it over to the Jeep and poured the water over the engine, which hissed and sizzled like a fajita platter. There was more smoke, lots of it, but at least the flames were out.

We all had a good laugh as we made our way onto the field for practice that day, but in my heart, I knew I was done with that Jeep. A week or so later I traded it in for a truck. Pulling the keys out of the ignition for the last time was a small but necessary heartbreak, but I honestly never looked back. The Jeep's purpose was to get me from place to place, and once it couldn't, it was time to move on.

There's a lot of comfort to be found in familiarity. I'm that way with some things. I've always been passionate about loyalty, especially when it comes to my nonnegotiables—my marriage, my family, my faith, and who I am at my core. Still, I refuse to settle for the status quo.

When you think about it, life's essential nature is change. It's really the one constant we can all count on. Tomorrow will be different from today. Next season will look unlike where you find yourself right now. And so, every year when the snow clears, instead of moping around trying to sled on slushy patches of grass, you move into the next season of your life. As much as you enjoyed those crisp winter days, you don't want to wear snow boots in August to try to bring that feeling back. That would be a poor simulation of winter. Pretty much everyone would agree with that, but for some reason when it comes to relationships, we have the idea that acknowledging that one has run its course somehow dishonors that relationship. We follow the misguided assumption that loyalty always means sticking with someone no matter what, but I think the opposite can be true too. I'm not talking about your marriage here, but when it comes to relationships that aren't nonnegotiables, sometimes honoring someone looks like letting them go.

In your network you've got your ride-or-die, lifelong, thick-or-thin connections. The people who are with you through it all. You might change, and so might they, but you adapt. Being open to change and growth is like the secret elixir to really healthy relationships. We are pretty good at accepting that we ourselves are going to grow and change, but where we slip up is granting that same favor to others. Perhaps a friendship or relationship was bonded by a shared interest, political convictions, or faith, but then as life evolved, one person's relationship to those things changed. Our tendency is to act like the relationship hasn't. We'd prefer to just freeze people in time.

But when you can step back and release yourself from the idea that everybody in your life needs to stay in the same role forever, you open up so many doors, so many ways a person can walk into and out of your life—and sometimes, after some change, they walk back in. And each time they do, they show you something new.

Take Alissa. I met this young woman when I was hunting down tenants for some of my properties. Every day they were vacant was money down the drain, so I used to literally drive up and down the streets of Waco trying to find people to rent the darn things. The way Alissa tells it, some old guy hollered at her and her friends from the window of his truck asking if they needed a place to live. I tease her now about "stranger danger," because they actually responded, took their chances, and agreed to check the place out.

Not long after Alissa became our tenant, Jo and I asked her if she ever did any babysitting, and she did. When we saw how great she was with the kiddos, we asked her back again and again until she basically became part of the family, loving on our babies like they were her own. But the time came when Jo was stepping back from work for a bit, and we didn't need Alissa to help out with the kids anymore. We closed that chapter, but it wasn't long before we opened another. We hired her to work at the shop on Bosque, back before the Silos were open, where she quickly became one of our most valuable employees. Here's the great part, though: these days, Alissa is like our right-hand woman. We brought her on in a marketing position at Magnolia, and now she is an all-star. If I had held on to my idea of her as a sweet young lady who was there to help with my kids, I never would have found out what a boss she is, and our company would be worse off for it.

Alissa is an example of someone who grew alongside us. There are also times you'll find there are people in your network whose hearts naturally want to grow in a whole other direction. In those cases, hard as it may seem, you need to cut ties to let that happen.

In my first few years in construction, I hired a guy I'll call Jarrod.[1] He was my first foreman-type employee, and I was all fired up about him. I thought, *Man, this guy is going to take my construction company to the next level. Let's do this!*

Jarrod and I got off to a good start, we kicked a little butt, and for a while I was feeling pretty good about the way things were going. But as time passed, I started to notice that there were some things that weren't quite right. It was not about his work ethic. It definitely wasn't about his effort. It was more about his approach. I'm a fast mover, and Jarrod was *very thorough*. He worked at such a methodical pace that I felt like I was going to jump out of my skin waiting for him to finish. I had the big picture in mind and wanted to get the foundational work done and then circle back to finish out in a punch list—one, two, three. He wanted to get every little thing perfect before we could move on. My rabbit and his tortoise were always in two totally different places. We were working the same job, but we weren't working together.

When you work in construction, turnover is part of the business. But most of the time, when people had left my company it was because they had another opportunity or we both agreed it wasn't working out. With Jarrod, we had totally different views of the situation. He thought things were going great, and, well, I just didn't see it that way. I wrestled with how to break it to him for a while, thinking to myself, *Shoot. He's a good man. A family man who works hard, but we are just not jiving. How am I going to ever let this guy go?* Each Monday, I'd resolve to talk to him by the end of the week.

Well, Friday would come, Friday would go, and I wouldn't do it. This went on for *months*. I'd always thought that you stick by your people, no matter what, so I kept that relationship stumbling along.

Eventually, it got ridiculous. I am not a scared person. There is very little I'm afraid of, so I psyched myself up for it, gave myself a pep talk, figuring it couldn't be as bad as I'd imagined. I was right. It wasn't. It was *worse*.

Jarrod came in, and I said, "Jarrod, I'm sorry. I don't even know how to say this, but today's going to be your last day. To be honest with you, it's been a little bit of time coming." Well, this poor guy turned his back to me awkwardly, not in a disrespectful way, but in a totally humiliated way. He pulled out his keys and his cell phone and put them both on my desk. No eye contact, no shaking hands; he just mumbled something like, "Sorry if I disappointed you. I'll try better next time." And he walked out. That was the last I ever saw of Jarrod.

It was such a terrible experience. It was sad for me, it was sad for him, it was just sad, period. He was an employee and I was an employer, and it was pretty natural in that sense, but my heart felt like it got ripped out of my chest. It took a while for me to recover. Eventually though, I realized I hadn't been doing Jarrod any favors by keeping him on for those extra months.

One of the saddest things in the world to me is when something is keeping someone from fulfilling their purpose on this planet. Was Jarrod's purpose to frustrate me? No! As far as I could tell, it was to do good, thorough work for someone who appreciated it—or maybe it was to learn to paint or do customer service or coach his kid's swim team, who knows. In any case, every second I kept him on the job, I was keeping him from finding out where he belonged. As the saying goes, "A weed is just a flower growing in the wrong place." There's a lot of wisdom in that. If I had called Jarrod into my office months earlier, he would have been able to put down roots somewhere where he could thrive that much sooner.

Sometimes honoring someone looks like letting them go. #makesense

If we would all look out for one another's best interests, I believe in my heart the world would be a whole lot better place. Both people become freer to travel their own paths if we're not stuck holding on to each other when those paths diverge. Best-case scenario, you walk together for a spell, and then your path goes one way and theirs goes another, and you wish each other a good journey. If something isn't working out, you owe it to them to honor their calling, their gift, by letting them pursue it without you, and give yourself the freedom to honor your own.

The same goes for careers that have run their course and are no longer fulfilling you. A few months ago, Jo and I read an article in the *New York Times Magazine* written by an acclaimed chef who'd been running a restaurant in the Lower East Side of Manhattan for twenty years. She described her original vision for the place as "an intimate dinner party that [she] would throw every night in this charming, quirky space." Customers came back as much for the food as the feeling.

But, over the years, the neighborhood started to gentrify and the clientele changed. There were still plenty of grateful regulars, but there were also new people who didn't even bother to make eye contact with the hostess. Soon, the restaurant was overrun with people who were more focused on blasting out pictures of their food than enjoying it. When COVID-19 hit, she confronted the hard choice so many small businesses had to make: either continue limping along with a restaurant that didn't have that same intimate, dinner-with-friends feeling that had meant so much to her or do what had previously been unfathomable and shutter the restaurant. She could have accepted her friends' offer to raise cash with a GoFundMe campaign, or she could have filled out all the paperwork for the Paycheck Protection Program, but it was clear that the restaurant she'd opened was not the restaurant she'd be saving.

She decided to take it off life support. *Twenty years* she poured her heart into that business. I can only imagine how difficult it was to let it go. But she knew that if what remained was going to be a pale imitation, the way to honor her original vision and all the years the restaurant had brought her joy was to shut it down. As soon as she made that hard call, she immediately found herself dreaming about a new restaurant, one that got her excited to open again, full of people around large tables, boisterous and intimate at the same time. By deciding to let go, her arms were free to welcome something new.[2]

The power of honoring an experience by ending it hit Jo and me in a really personal way as we entered our fifth season of *Fixer Upper*. We'd jumped into that whole experience with both feet, breath held, and we made a heck of a splash. We got so much joy from our time on the show, and it totally transformed our lives and our business.

I hinted a little bit in chapter 5 about how I'd started to feel unsettled toward the end, but the truth is I felt more than unsettled. Now, I don't want you to get the wrong idea from the car story at the beginning of this chapter. Nothing exploded. No one set anything on fire. But the signs that our run had ended felt every bit as clear to me as smoke rising from under the hood.

I didn't know this about the television business, but when you get a hit like, say, *American Idol*, within a very short period of time you get shows like *The Voice, X Factor, America's Got Talent, Masked Singer,* and probably a dozen others I'm forgetting—shows that seem an awful lot like *American Idol*. Networks take a proven formula and run with it, so when our show sort of took off and they saw how America was responding to Jo and me, it seemed like they wanted to find other couples who went around knocking things down and then building them up again. But *Fixer Upper* wasn't a formula where you could plug in a new number and get the same result. It was our *lives*.

Our whole deal is authenticity, so when we thought about the possibility of an army of Chip and Jo lookalikes out there, it felt a little like looking in those wraparound mirrors where you see copies of your reflection reaching on for miles. Even the most grounded person can start to wonder, *Wait a minute, which one am I? Is that one me, twenty-two back? Or am I the first one?* Once there's a bunch of duplicates out there, it can be hard to spot the original among them.

Over those five years, Jo and I had grown. After our initial couple (okay, maybe it was a dozen) episodes, we started to get the hang of doing the show. I stopped making excuses to talk to the camera people and got my butt *in front* of the camera where I was supposed to be. Jo came out of her shell and, whoa, she was a natural. There is something built into the very fabric of my wife that is quietly compelling and is meant to be shared with the world. She's a visionary in every sense of the word. You can't imagine the pride I felt watching her tap into her potential the way she was.

We were both honored to have the chance to be invited into families' lives and be part of their stories. And after a while, by season three or four, we were ready to take some risks but were told to stay the course, which was, in the producers' minds, perfectly good enough.

I'm a feeler. When something penetrates my skin, it gets inside and affects me right down to my bones. Having people tell me what to do, where to be, what to wear, how to act—well, there was little of me left by the end of the day. Jo and I both knew we still should have been thrilled—after all, ratings were great, and every season was more successful than the last. But we just weren't. By the end, we were on autopilot. And you know by now how I feel about that.

I don't regret those five seasons of *Fixer Upper*—far from it. When I look back, I have these amazing, fond memories and deep gratitude, but it was like the Jeep. Everything about that Jeep was perfect. Until it wasn't. I knew I had outgrown it, but we'd been through so much together that it was hard to close the door for the last time.

The show and the people I worked with for those years challenged me in ways I couldn't have seen coming. The end result was that I walked away with an even greater appreciation for my nonnegotiables, especially my need to keep growing and changing and to hold fast to things that matter to Jo and me at our core.

REWRITE AN ENDING

We have all had a relationship that didn't end well, whether it was with a person or an organization. Chances are, though, it wasn't bad through and through. You were in it for a reason.

MAKE YOUR OWN HIGHLIGHT REEL. What were some of the good parts of your relationship? How did you benefit from it? What did you enjoy?

REWRITE THE ENDING. If you had another shot at it, how could your relationship have ended in a way that honored both of you? Could you rewrite the story? Call for a do-over by writing a letter, sending an email, or, heck, calling this person up on the phone and acknowledging the peaks of your experience together.

When we made the decision to call it on the show, it was so important to us that we honored everything that we were supposed to do to finish out the season. We gave it our all up until the very last episode because I've come to believe that how you end things is as important as how you begin them. When we think back on something, we don't remember every single part of an experience. We mostly remember two parts—the most extreme part, good or bad, and the end. You can have the world's best time at the state fair eating corn dogs, listening to the band, and getting dizzy on the Ferris wheel, but if you drop your ice cream on your shirt and get stuck in traffic on the way home, that's going to tint the whole day. Psychologists call this the "peak-end rule." The way we remember things is like the way an editor puts together a highlight reel—it's made up of the really big moments, the highest highs, the lowest lows, and the big finale.[3] A kicker who misses what could have been the game-winning field goal is going to feel like crap even if he hit every other attempt and walked away with a twelve-point game. On the other hand, maybe he doesn't mind so much that he tanked one mid-game if he also put a sixty-yarder through the uprights to win it.

Our internal narrators have great storytelling instincts. Those narrators know that endings matter. Endings linger and define how you remember something. We can't always control the peak part of our experiences or relationships with someone in our network, but we usually have some control over how the end plays out. You've got a choice: you can let a relationship or experience run its course until it sputters out, or you can write your own ending, and in the process honor the journey that got you there.

BOTTOM LINE

Hold on to each other but don't hold each other back.

CHAPTER 13

GREAT(ER) EXPECTATIONS

Jo and I have a group of close friends who have all been a part of each other's lives for years. We've seen one another through getting married, starting businesses, expanding families, gaining a few pounds, losing a few hairs, and all the joy and heartbreak in between. The group of us spent the first day of 2020 together in New Orleans. We'd traveled there to watch our Baylor Bears play against the Georgia Bulldogs in the Sugar Bowl. It was only the second time in Bears' history they'd been in the Sugar Bowl, and we were *pumped* about being there. The night before the game we all went out for a nice dinner to unwind and enjoy one another's company.

Going out to eat in New Orleans is a kick. They really do know how to let the good times roll. Not only is the food delicious but dinner felt like a party, and our whole crew was swept up in it. That's when I decided it would be a good time to jump in and shake things up a bit.

"So," I asked the group, "how would your lives be different if fear wasn't part of the equation?"

I looked around the table to see my friends looking back at me like *Who invited this buzzkill?* But gradually, they spoke up. They talked about things they would do in a heartbeat if they weren't afraid of the potential collateral damage, if life's expectations (even good ones) weren't there.

I couldn't believe what I was hearing. People I'd known for decades, people who have it together—nice life, solid marriage, great kids—had been harboring all these neglected dreams. I listened, inspired, as they began to articulate them, some for the very first time. These were people I knew well. We'd had plenty of deep conversations over the years, but I'd never heard *any* of this. The honesty at the table that night was something special.

I sat back in my chair and let it wash over me. As accomplished and energetic as these folks were, the list of things they weren't doing was astonishing. But equally surprising was that these dear friends of mine had accepted that it was okay not to be doing them.

I know the people at that table aren't the only ones living with unexplored dreams. I have nothing against feeling grateful for your blessings, but *why not* expect something more, something greater? I want to live in a world where people's dreams are playing out more regularly, not hindered by fear. I want people in my network to chase after those dreams, to expect greater.

THE MASTER SABOTEUR

When it comes to expecting great things from ourselves, fear is public enemy number one—a master saboteur. For one thing, fear zaps our energy. It's the mental gauntlet we have to run before we even reach the starting line. We spend so much energy worrying that we won't get it right that we're not starting with a full tank. For another, fear is limiting.

Even if we have the energy, it locks us in place like a horse at the starting gate.

There are two main kinds of fear: fear of something bad happening and fear of the unknown, or as psychologists call them, "risk aversion" and "ambiguity aversion." The first one involves the feeling when your mind and your body shout in unison, "Don't open that door!" That's the primal sensation that has developed to help keep us from putting ourselves in mortal danger. If you decide not to free solo a four-hundred-foot-high rock face because you're afraid that you're going to end up a pile of blood and bones, I'm not going to talk you out of listening to that kind of essential fear intended to protect your physical safety. It's the more common mental or emotional fear of something bad happening—aka failure—that I want to pick on. We're afraid of failure—or, more likely, we're afraid of being *seen* as a failure. And that, well, that I have to challenge.

Most of the time the actual failure part is not really all that frightening. It's the anticipation that scares the heck out of us. Ridley Scott knew this when he made the choice not to let the audience see the monster too often in his movie *Alien*. He told *Variety*, "The best screening room in the world is the space between your ears."[1]

That sounds exactly right to me. Fear lives between our ears. Our ability to imagine the future is one of our great skills, but we sometimes give ourselves too much artistic license, imagining bad scenarios that will cause us to doubt ourselves and freeze us in place.

We do what William Paul Young, author of *The Shack*, calls "future tripping."[2] We leap ahead to the consequences of an action, letting our fear-based mindset dictate what those consequences will be. In the confines of our own mind, we can create absolute but unfounded certainty about how something will go down. *If I try to talk to her, she's going to blow me off. I'm not important enough for her to talk to.* Or *Who am I to try to sell this thing I've been making in my garage? Everyone will think I'm full of myself.* As Young points out, we humans are insistently drawn to that certainty. But magic lives in mystery, whether it's in your relationships, your career, or your spiritual life. It's like we've become so attached to a protective mindset that we're being helicopter parents to ourselves, not allowing for a single bump or bruise along the way, and in the process stifling joy, creativity, and possibility. That's no way to live. We have to learn to let mystery reign when it comes to what *could* happen instead of fearing it.

There are hundreds of ways the kind of fear that stops you cold can manifest itself. Why don't we just get a few of them out on the table right now?

You're afraid you have no talent.

You're scared of what you have to lose.

You're embarrassed about your dreams.

You're afraid of the consequences.

You're afraid of letting people down.

You're afraid people will laugh at you.

You're afraid of failing.

You're afraid that you have wasted your life.

You're afraid you don't have enough time.

You're afraid you don't have the money.

You're afraid people will resent you.

You're afraid you won't fit in.

Or like me, you're afraid of getting lost in the crowd.

Of course all of these are possible, but are they *likely?* Or have you let your imagination get the best of you? Now let me ask you this: Is there anything you could do to lessen the chance your fear comes to pass—*besides* not trying?

If you're not ready for that kind of jump right now, then I'll ask you to do this exercise with me:

FEAR FACT-FINDING

We all have fears that haunt us. The first step in robbing fear of its power is to name it. Make your own list of fears that are holding you back. Rate the chances that your fear will actually happen on a scale of 1 to 5. Then act like a scientist and ask yourself, *What are the facts?* Do you have data to support your analysis, or are you letting your imagination fuel those fears?

Fear	How likely it is to happen	Facts

Many times the reason we don't have high expectations for ourselves (or others) is simply because we are lulled by comfort. It's more convenient and an awful lot easier to stay in our lane and follow instructions. But we won't ever get to where we want to go if we're operating with those kinds of shackles around our ankles. My question is, Why aren't we just as afraid of living without passion as we are of living without certainty? Are we sure that the safe place is actually safe, or is it simply familiar?

Fear is a parasite that has wormed its way into our brains. But it can't live without us as a host, and we've got to stop feeding it in order to get rid of it. And the best way to starve fear is to change your mindset. Get active in how you engage with fear instead of accepting its presence in your life.

Let's not give fear a free pass. Interrogate it. Ask it what it really is, what it's doing in your life, and where it came from. How much of what you're afraid of is actually based in reality? What are you risking when you capitulate to fear? What could you gain if fear was not a factor?

Now, let's turn to the fear of the unknown. This one requires a closer look. It's not inherently bad, but it does need better branding.

The unknown is where possibility hangs out. It can be tough to spot untapped possibility because we've trained ourselves to expect life to be predictable—push this button, pull that lever, get the same result. Often when we look to the future, that's all we see: more of the same. In much the same way, an unpursued passion or dream can be intimidating because you don't know a thing about what your life would look like or how it would have to change if you invited that dream in.

Why aren't we just as afraid of living without passion as we are of living without certainty? #makesense

What could you do to change that? For starters, you could get more familiar mentally with what it would be like if you were to take the risk. Talk to folks who have done whatever it is you're fantasizing about—whether it's starting a new business, quitting your job, or learning a new skill. Take one step. Do some research. Take a class. Heck, watch a single YouTube video. Do the work so you can cross "unknown" off your list of reasons not to expect greater.

If Jo and I had stuck to what we knew, we would never be where we are today. When we started filming *Fixer Upper* the first time around, very quickly it became clear that those supposed twenty extra hours a week were going to be more like sixty. Filming schedule aside, our home renovation business was growing fast, and our little shop on Bosque had lines out the door. Overnight, Jo and I found ourselves with not one but three full-time jobs. I have a high tolerance for multitasking, but those days were insane. Just doing one of those jobs well would've been more than enough for Jo and me to tackle by ourselves (while raising our four young kids). Our needs were endless, and I knew we couldn't navigate them alone.

But I'm a serial optimist. Tell me something is impossible, and I start to look at it with a whole lot of interest. Tell me someone isn't capable, and I become the dude in the *Karate Kid* ready to prove to the world that anybody can do anything. Don't get me wrong—if someone yells that there's an iceberg ahead, it's not that I can't see the large ice cap emerging from the water fifty yards in front of us, because, well, I'm not blind. I'll just be the one to also point out that calmer seas await on the other side.

Early on, my ridiculously high expectations emerged strictly out of necessity. In those days, fear would have been a luxury. Things were moving so quickly there just wasn't enough time for anyone to *become* afraid. Jo and I expected greater for ourselves and the people in our network. I'd ask the folks on our team to do a million different tasks, some of them way out of their comfort zone. For our employees, in merely attempting something utterly beyond their experience, they dragged themselves into new dimensions, and in the process learned something about themselves and what they're capable of, just like Jo and I had. Expecting greater became part of our company's DNA. Years later, when we started our magazine, *Magnolia Journal*, the most experience any of us had with magazines was as a subscriber. But when the opportunity came our way, we looked at the people in our network and fully trusted that we could figure it out together.

It was a bumpy road in the beginning. Our advisors kept trying to shoehorn us into a preexisting format that was very sellable, and the easy thing would have been to listen to them. After all, they were the experts. Why were we trying to reinvent the wheel? But in our guts we knew that what we wanted was something different—a magazine that felt like it was going back to basics. We wouldn't cheap out on paper or bulk it up with ads. We would offer what we knew people liked best about us—something authentic and relatable, a return to something that felt essential, something real. There were a lot of really good reasons for it not to work. But it did. In an era where publications are folding, *Magnolia Journal* has thrived. Oh, and we put that first issue out in like two months. Nobody told us that was next to impossible until after it was on newsstands. If we had listened to other people's expectations, *Magnolia Journal* wouldn't exist.

Magnolia didn't just survive; we *thrived* because we pushed fear aside. That season of insanity deepened my faith in human potential and in the talents of people who are given extraordinary challenges and then the space to outperform them. Honestly, a lot of times it was a matter of me getting out of the way so our team could go to town on their own.

This crash course in business from the trenches convinced me of the age-old adage "Iron sharpens iron." Not only did I want greater expectations for myself, I also wanted them for those who worked with and for me.

Maybe you're thinking, *Chip, that's nice and all, but isn't it, like, basic math that the higher the threshold, the greater the margin for error or flat-out failure?*

Maybe, but that's not the way I choose to see it. For me, the higher the threshold, the further you're bound to aim. And even if you don't hit your target, I guarantee you made it a lot further than you would have shooting at close range.

But it's not even the end result that matters to me. What I'm hoping to see from our team is a willingness to take the shot.

We met Becki when she had brand-new triplets. It wasn't long before she became a close friend, our families bonding over having a mess of kids to take care of. We learned early on in our friendship that she is also an amazing cook. Every January, Jo and I start our year off right by going to Whit and Becki's house to celebrate the New Year and enjoy a ham, black-eyed peas, and a bunch of sides that we always eat our weight in.

When we decided to open our restaurant, we knew we'd need someone to run the thing. We immediately thought of Becki. She'd had a food background and owned a restaurant before she'd started at her current job with a nonprofit, and we sure loved her cooking. It was just a matter of convincing her to take the shot.

We texted her on a Friday night and asked, "What time do your kids go to bed?" We told her we'd like to come over and run something by her. While her kids were sleeping, we explained that we had bought a historic café in Waco that we wanted to open as a new restaurant, and we needed someone to run it. Becki set some kind of record for the fastest time ever for turning down a job offer. She loved the job she already had. It gave her the flexibility she needed with four-year-old triplets. For sure she would not be giving it up to start a restaurant.

But we're drawn to Becki for a reason, and it's not just the New Year's spread. She's someone who feels the pull of the unknown. Despite how adamant she was, Jo and I could see that we'd set some wheels turning. After a minute, she asked, "Just theoretically, what do you want to serve?"

I knew she was in. It took a month or so to fully convince her to leave her safe job for something unsure, but eventually she signed on. In the time Becki has been with Magnolia, she has not only handled the restaurant and the bakery but also helped with all of our food entities, including working with Jo to develop recipes for her cookbooks, generating a lot of the food content for the magazine, and on top of it all, taking on an added responsibility for our coffee shop. What might have sounded impossible or flat-out insane, Becki has met with smarts and spirit.

Becki is living proof around here of what it looks like to continually expect greater for yourself. Because of her willingness to lean into the unknown, our team has been able to experience the reward that comes with a leap of faith like that.

Over the years Jo and I have crafted our expectations for our team, creating four pillars of our Magnolia creed: grit, learning, ownership, and the word "impossible." Not to sound like Willy Wonka, but when people step into our world, we truly want them to believe in the impossible. And by that we mean we don't want them to stop at the status quo. We want them to try something new, to experiment, to rewrite the rules and see if they can't dream something into being. As long as someone tries, failure is no big deal to me. Most wounds heal, and most problems (even self-inflicted ones) can be fixed. It's not as much the result as the journey that I'm concerned with.

For some people this concept might sound counterintuitive, or maybe even counterproductive. Conventional wisdom would say you're better off starting from a place of possibility. Begin with what's reasonable, and then go from there. Surely it's a smart use of resources and man-hours, and it doesn't necessarily yield lousy results. But that's not the way we've chosen to do things. We've found that people are empowered and inspired by the fact that we refuse to simply go through the motions. And when we allow our people to stretch out and try something new, it only drives them to see how much further they can go.

We are all prone to self-fulfilling prophecies. Tell yourself you don't have what it takes to do something interesting with your life and you can rest assured that you won't. Say you're willing to take a chance on a *greater* version of what others consider a reasonably possible reality, well, at least now you're giving yourself a shot. It comes down to this wisdom from Henry Ford: "Whether you believe you can do a thing or not, you're right."[3]

My point is that you can't let fear lead. Give that role to your instinct, your intuition. The moment you're willing to say that you're not afraid to fail, to falter, to come up short, to [fill in the blank], fear loses its power over you. Sure, you may very well fail. You could fall short.

Or.. you just might succeed.

I hope that, like our friends that night in New Orleans, you'll voice your own passions that are stirring inside you and allow them to drive you. Take a chance, write the book, start a company, heal that relationship, or run that marathon you've been talking about. I can't promise that the pursuit of "greater" won't involve certain discomforts. For the most part, my own network has had my back when I've gone all-in on a few gambles. But if I'm being honest here, there were times doubters chose to keep their distance. There were even a few who made themselves comfortable on the sidelines just to see how it all played out before they decided if and when to start coming around again.

It can be lonely to take a risk, or to choose to pursue something unfamiliar to those around you. Operating outside the norm makes people uncomfortable, even those closest to you, because no one wants to see someone they care about fail. And some people just plain and simple don't want to be associated with failure, even if it's not their own.

When you bet on someone in your own network, don't lose sight of what it is you're really rooting for. 'Cause it's not their idea. It's them. That way failure is no big deal.

So dream big, shake up preexisting ideas, take risks, and encourage those around you to do the same. Ask yourself what might come if fear wasn't part of the equation—and then expect something great.

BOTTOM LINE

Fear Sux! Trust your instincts + intuition to guide you toward the risks worth taking.

CHAPTER 14

FIXER-UPPER MENTALITY

Here we go again, I thought as my mom walked through the door to my classroom with a look on her face that made it clear this was not how she wanted to spend her afternoon. I could relate.

I must have been in fourth or fifth grade, but this wasn't my first time in an after-school conference about my academic performance. Mom sat down next to me, facing my teacher, who was waiting in silence, hands folded in front of her on a big gray metal desk. I don't know if it's my memory or the reality, but I picture my teacher with a librarian bun perched high on her head and glasses perched low on her nose so she could peer at us over them.

I slumped lower in my chair as my teacher began. "Mrs. Gaines, I'm not going to beat around the bush. We're not sure Chip is going to be able to move on to the next grade. His grades are terrible. He's acting out in class.." She continued, but my attention had already left the building. I'd heard it all before—the mile-long list of my shortcomings as a student. She wasn't wrong. I might not have been the smartest kid in class, but I was definitely the most.. interesting. If I couldn't outperform the smart kids, I figured I might as well make them laugh. I talked a mile a minute during school—that is, of course, until I was called on to answer a question. That's when I'd duck my head down under my desk like I'd suddenly taken a real deep interest in my shoelaces.

My teacher finished up: "We need you to do more at home. Otherwise, he's going to have to repeat the grade."

I did what I always did at these things—nodded respectfully and promised to do better. My mom assured my teacher that this would be a team effort. And then we left, the embarrassment on my mom's face a deep sting for a kid who really did want to please his parents.

The thing is, I never felt dumb, exactly. I just felt confused by the idea that sitting in a chair and listening to a teacher was supposed to get my brain humming. Having someone talk *at me* was like handing a left-handed kid a pair of right-handed scissors and expecting him to cut straight. And yet, it seemed like it was working for everyone else. Were they *actually* interested in the fact that two plus two equals six?

If it wasn't for the time I spent with my grandfather, J.B., I might have grown up thinking I was a person who wasn't meant for learning.

A PERSON WHO..

Go get yourself a piece of paper and fill out this prompt:

I am a person who..

You can write as many answers as you feel like, and they can be good, bad, so-so. That's right; even the best qualities can keep you from growing if you hold on to them too tightly as a fixed part of your identity.

Now think of a time when whatever quality you chose held you back—maybe you didn't volunteer for a new community organization because you think of yourself as a person who is not politically active even though you care passionately about the place where you live.

Identify a small action that *a person who* was politically active might have taken. Could you imagine yourself doing that? Often we can't imagine ourselves taking on a new identity, but we can imagine doing a single action.

We do this a lot. We start to think of ourselves as "a person who..": *I'm a person who is not good at math. A person who doesn't have what it takes. A person who isn't funny enough.* Maybe we decided it for ourselves, but more likely it came from other people's expectations, and it results in an "as is" mentality, or what psychologists would call a "fixed mindset," a term popularized by Stanford professor Carol Dweck.[1] People with this mentality think that you are born with a certain amount of gifts, and you get what you get. No matter what you do or how hard you try, your gifts remain unchanged.

There was no room for "as is" on J.B.'s ranch. Going out there was like someone had switched my world from black and white to Technicolor. On the ranch I became "a person who.. believed anything is possible."

J.B. was a man of few words. As I was growing up, I was on his ranch as much as time and my parents would allow. The place was heaven on earth for me, with its wide blue skies yawning over acres and acres of red dirt and low green grasses that encircled a murky pond for watering the animals, which we Texans call a "tank." In the summers I'd stay there for weeks, just me and J.B. We'd get up so early that sometimes you could still see a glint of moonlight shimmering on the grass as our boots kicked up the dew.

One summer, when I was in eighth grade, J.B. and I were out sweating buckets as we rode his horses in the late morning sun. (When it gets hot in Texas, it's one hundred degrees, and for some reason this little town of Archer City, where my granddad lived, is always hotter than the rest of the state.) We'd been out riding all morning, and it showed. We headed in, and J.B. stroked his horse's neck like he was taking its temperature and said, "We've got to get these horses some water."

I said, "Yes sir. What do I need to do?"

J.B. turned his horse down toward the tank to get him a drink, and I followed suit.

I didn't know it then, but when you lead a horse to water you have to be *very* clear with that animal to stop right where his front feet step into the tank, because if he gets two feet in, and then gets two more feet in, he doesn't think you're leading him to a drink of water—he thinks you're leading him to a bath.

Well, I didn't know that. J.B.'s horse stopped right where he needed to stop for a well-deserved drink, and my horse walked in right behind him, *clomp clomp clomp*. When he realized his rider wasn't giving him the slightest resistance, he took a couple more steps, a couple more steps, and before I knew what was happening, the horse sat down and started to roll over—with me still on him.

In zero seconds flat, I was pinned underwater beneath this horse's tummy with no idea what was going on. The horse stayed under the water for a few seconds, came up for air, and then the dang thing rolled again. By this point, J.B. had hopped off his horse and was knee-deep in the tank. He grabbed the reins and pulled that poor old horse out of the water, while I was still trying to figure out which way was up.

J.B. didn't sit me down for a lecture about horse safety. And he didn't forbid me from hopping right back into the saddle. He trusted I'd gotten the point. J.B. would have agreed with George Bernard Shaw who said, "If you teach a man anything he will never learn it."[2]

My grandfather let me figure it out for myself. And you better believe I never let a horse wade into a tank again.

There are certain lessons that can't be taught in a book. You can't go to college for them. You can't study them. You learn them through experiences that sink down and settle into your bones. Those experiences on the ranch were the exact opposite of being inside a classroom. I was learning, growing, and changing—except now I felt like I'd been scraped down to my core, totally alive, electric with excitement. That's who I was when I was with J.B.: a wild thing set free.

One of my least favorite phrases in the English language is "That's the way it's always been done." My response to that is "So what?" When you learn something for yourself, you learn it with the passion of a convert. You're not passively receiving wisdom. You're out there with a bow and arrow hunting it down and then wrestling it to the ground. You can't help but have a greater respect for the thing when you've tackled it yourself. You've earned a deeper knowledge of what it's all about. You get back to basics, learning from the inside out, when instead of doing things the way you've been told to do them, you poke and prod and go, "Hey, what if we tried it this way?" It might be harder than just sitting back and letting muscle memory kick in, but the payoff is that it becomes almost primal.

It wasn't until college that I met the first educator who didn't think I was a total idiot. His name was Dr. Jeff Tanner. (Yep, the same Dr. Tanner who would eventually try to set me up with the copier sales job.) When I first met him, something clicked. I took his course on sales, and he saw something in me that gave me the first stroke of confidence I ever had inside the four walls of a classroom.

There were kids in his class who were economics majors and math majors, kids whose parents were doctors and lawyers, whose paths to a corner office seemed all but guaranteed. But as the semester went on, Dr. Tanner called on me more and more frequently. He'd somehow heard about time I'd spent as a book salesman for a company called Southwestern, so when he needed an example, he looked past the rich kid who'd spent his summer as a part-time lifeguard at the country club, to me.

He'd say, "Chip, why don't you give us an example of what sales looks like in the real world?" And I'd say, "Well, all right. Two years ago I was in Troy, Michigan, where I didn't know a soul. I had to march myself into a convenience store to ask for directions to figure out where to go to ask someone where to live so that I could hit the streets and sell books door-to-door." I'd tell stories about my experiences, and Dr. Tanner loved it. Where other educators had seen a restless cutup, he saw that there was more to me than a smart aleck. I was a doer, and Dr. Tanner recognized the value in that. He saw that I went after things and I wasn't afraid to fail. He was using a different measuring tool to estimate my ability. I think what he might've seen in me was what I call a *fixer-upper mentality*.

Early in our marriage, when I was just getting started with my construction business, I bought a house without telling Jo. It was a little A-frame on ten acres of land with big trees all around the property. It was modest, which is a nice way of saying that it needed a lot of TLC. I thought Jo was going to be over the moon when she saw it, so I did this big, elaborate thing where I got a blindfold and had her put it on. When I pulled up to the field, I took the blindfold off and gestured with my arms like a magician doing his big reveal: *Ta-da!* I turned to Jo and said, "Look, babe, this is our next project! We got it! Let's do this!"

I thought my new wife was going to be overjoyed and I was going to come off looking like a genius. But Jo took one look at that house and all she saw was a black hole of needs. She didn't ask me how much I'd bought it for, or how much it would take to improve it, or how much we could sell it for. She just stood there and burst into tears.

Okay, I thought, *maybe she just needs to see the inside to get a sense of the potential.*

So we walked in the front door. Because the power had been cut off for a week or so, the food in the fridge had rotted, and the smell slugged us in the face like a boxer. I had to finish the rest of the inspection myself because Jo had already given up and was waiting in the car. When I got back in beside her, she looked at me like I had just run over a dog, like buying this investment property was cruel and unusual punishment. She saw the house as it was—a dump—but I saw it as it could be after I ripped the carpet out, cleaned the fridge, and primed the thing. It could be a beauty, a fixer upper.

That's how I see most people—full of potential, not set in stone. My fixer-upper mentality has made me a lifelong learner, and I've filled my network with people who share that mindset, people who believe in potential—especially their own. (For the record, Jo can spot potential a mile away. She's just a little more careful than I am about the holes we might step in if we rush in too quickly.)

As humans, our untapped potential is *insane*. Back in 1905, Einstein figured out that matter is energy waiting to happen. If you are average-sized, you contain enough energy to explode with the force of a couple dozen hydrogen bombs if you could just figure out how to release it.[3] Just think about how much potential is in our *brain* matter. Activate it, and the impact will blow you away. The way to light the fuse is to believe in your power to do so, to believe in what Dweck calls the "power of yet."[4] With this kind of mindset, when you encounter a roadblock, you don't stop short. Instead you say to yourself, "I can't do that.. *yet.*" You know that with a little effort and a lot of tries, you can develop new abilities just like you can build muscle. You stretch a little and try it out and do it until you fail, and then you come back stronger the next day. You're not focused on the goal of winning. You're focused on the process of getting stronger and wiser, of being capable of more today than you were yesterday. The first step is just believing that potential is there. Doing that changes everything.

Imagine waking up in the morning with an "as is" mentality. You gulp down your coffee and head for the office before your spouse is even awake. You space out until you hit the parking lot. During a meeting, your boss asks if anyone has anything to add. Briefly, you consider sharing an idea you had, but before you even put your hand up, you check yourself, thinking, *Who am I to suggest this? It's outside my area of expertise. Better stick to what I know.* So you go back to your desk and do the rest of your job in your sleep, only coming to your senses long enough to check the clock, 'cause surely it's almost 5:00 p.m. by now. When you get home and your spouse asks you, "How was your day?" you answer, "Same as yesterday. Fine." And that's exactly what it was—fine. Fine? "Fine" is okay for "How was the dentist?" But this is *your life* we're talking about. "Fine" shouldn't even be on the table.

Let's look at what happens if you have a fixer-upper mentality. You wake up and have a cup of coffee with your spouse, who mentions something interesting they heard on the radio. You tune in on your way to the office and it gets your wheels spinning. During a meeting, your boss asks if anyone has anything to add, and your hand is already in the air. You share a thought you had this morning about how to do something a little differently, or maybe a lot differently. You might not have all the details worked out, but that's okay—you can always figure that part out later. You head back to your desk and "later" starts right now. You dig in, fired up by your idea, and before you know it, the day is over. You head home with your mental fuel tank still full, excited to share the details of your day, because today wasn't the same as yesterday. You have a feeling tomorrow won't be the same as today, and you can't wait to find out how. That's the difference a fixer-upper mentality can make.

If Jo and I had stayed content with an "as is" mindset all these years, so much of the life we've built and the work we've come to love just wouldn't exist.

That's the kind of challenge that gets me up in the morning, because I know I'm going to learn something along the way. The chance that we might blow it is part of the magic. The first ten things we try might fail, but then I can keep those lessons in my pocket for next time. That's my idea of a business plan. For me, even if it goes up in smoke, it's never a total loss. If you're going for it and moving forward, sure, it's probably going to cost you something. But even if you lose, you've learned too. You can always grab a lesson from an opportunity, even one that didn't pan out exactly the way you'd hoped. That's the value of always moving, always pushing yourself instead of coasting along as you always have. That's why "We can do hard things" is a Gaines family mantra. Say it enough times and you start believing it.

Maybe right now you're saying, "But Chip, I'm forty, fifty years old. The time for this old dog to learn new tricks is long past." I've got good news for you. It turns out your brain can still grow and change in adult-hood, depending on how well you use it. In fact, the best thing you can do for your brain is to learn something new.

It's human nature to want to figure things out. There's a reason that the most common word you hear before "curious" is "naturally." We are born with a natural curiosity and restlessness. Despite what's commonly thought of as the good life—one where you're resting on a beach with a piña colada and a fat 401(k)—we are actually *happiest* when we are learning and growing. We don't like sitting around on our rumps doing nothing. There was even a study done about this where subjects were allowed to sit around twiddling their thumbs, but they got so bored that they gave themselves electric shocks instead of doing nothing.[5] I'll admit, if I'd been in that room, I might've been the one to come up with that idea.

The act of learning looks different for everyone. For some, it may look like trying something entirely new; for others it might mean just the opposite—the return to a project or skill you've stepped away from for a while, this time with fresh eyes. The key is to find something that matters to you. The things we know that make us who we are. Why would you ever want to quit learning what you can do or what you're capable of offering this world?

The first step is just believing that potential is there. #makesense

Do you want to hear something funny? You probably won't be surprised that when I graduated college, I vowed that I would never willingly box myself into the four walls of a classroom ever again. I had put that kind of learning in the category of "just not my thing." But then, in the summer of 2019, Jo and I were invited to be part of a class at Harvard Business School that would focus on the business of entertainment and media. When I pictured myself in that class, I immediately had flashbacks to those after-school conferences with my mom by my side and the teacher telling me I was a square peg. But it was freakin' Harvard, one of the most storied institutions in the world, and the class would focus on what we needed to know most at the time—*media as a business*. My fixer-upper mentality kicked in. We cleared our calendars and enrolled.

Some of my buddies thought it was hilarious that this former class clown would be rubbing elbows with some of the brightest young minds in the world. "Make sure you remember to pack a few clean shirts," they joked. Jo and I flew up to Boston the day before our sixteenth wedding anniversary and pushed back the first-day jitters as we took our seats.

Jo totally looked the part, perched at her desk like a cute teacher's pet, but I'll admit that I spent a few minutes looking around and wondering, *What am I doing here?* Not only was I in a classroom again but it was the king of classrooms, the *Harvard* of classrooms. And I wasn't some young hotshot. I was a fortysomething dude who had gotten a diploma by the skin of his teeth nearly two decades earlier. But once the professor got going, I realized I had as much to contribute—and as much to learn—as everyone else. I was *digging it*. The professor used Beyoncé's decision to defy conventional wisdom and drop her album *Lemonade*, complete with videos, all at once as a case study for ignoring the "how it's always been done" advice and doing it your own way—with spectacular results. Now *that's* what I was talking about. *That* I could learn from. My brain

cells were firing away. I could feel the thrill of this highly active form of learning activating my potential. I was starting to think that back in college I just hadn't been a good student.. *yet*. You know I celebrated the personal victory by buying every Harvard sweatshirt and coffee cup I could fit in my suitcase.

I don't mean to suggest that everyone should go back to school. I mean stay on your toes, stay invested, stay interested. There's an old business adage that says if you're not growing you're dying. That kind of talk gives me chills. The way I see it, growth by its very nature calls us out of an "as is" mentality by shaping and reshaping what we think we know to be true. So what about you? Are you going to be a person who accepts yourself as is? Or can you cultivate a fixer-upper mentality? Take a look at your attitude. At the end of each day, instead of looking at what you've accomplished, look at what you've *learned*. It'll make a world of difference.

BOTTOM LINE

"Smart" might come from watching + studying but Wisdom comes from doing, failing, + trying again.

CHAPTER 15

STUPID SMART

When Jo and I left *Fixer Upper*, we thought there was no way we would ever go back to the show. Well, if you've seen the lineup of shows that are launching our network, you might have noticed there are new episodes of.. *Fixer Upper*.

It might make more sense if I could tell you we made this decision after a very careful process where I drew a line down the middle of a sheet of paper. On one side I listed the pros and on the other side were the cons. Then I talked it through with a handful of trusted advisors before coming to a rational conclusion. Or it might make sense if I went off on a silent retreat and did a whole lot of soul-searching. Or that I practiced how I would bring the issue up with Jo in front of a full-length mirror so I could get the wording just right.

But that's not at all what it looked like. Overthinking is my kryptonite. If you give me a script, there's a 100 percent chance I'll screw it up. I'll mess up on a word, and then I can't remember the one after that, and then I can't read at all. Then it's just over.

Something I've learned is, simply put: Jo and I live and die by my spontaneity. And listen, I don't throw that "and die" part in there lightly. Sometimes I'll do something spontaneous and it is *miserable*. I screw up terribly and everybody is really affected, so I'm not saying it's always a success. But I've won enough times that people around me have learned to let me swing for the fences. When I make a quick call that seems like it comes out of nowhere, it may not always look smart, but that doesn't make it unwise. Not when it's a matter of my head, my heart, and my gut all working together as a unit. What I call *stupid smart*.

That's what happened when Jo and I decided to return to *Fixer Upper*.

We had just done a little promo piece for the network where I talked about how the show was our past, where we were, and the network was our future, where we were headed. I hadn't noticed it when we were filming, but when I watched the final spot, it hit me that our past and our future weren't moving in opposite directions at all; they were looping toward each other, coming full circle. That's when I said to Jo, "What if we did a few episodes of *Fixer Upper* and attached it to the network?"

When I blurted out my idea to return to *Fixer Upper*, I thought for sure that my level-headed wife was going to tell me that I was crazy. Instead, it didn't take but a minute for Jo to agree that a new season of *Fixer Upper* would be the perfect way to christen the network. We'd been working on putting together a roster of shows that focused on storytelling, on authenticity, and on getting back to basics. That lined up perfectly with what *Fixer Upper* had always meant to us at its best. We decided a new season on our very own network would feel like coming home.

I've made dozens of fly-by-the-seat-of-my-pants decisions in my life. Each time I do I am as at peace with my choice as I would have been had I weighed every option in a careful process. Till my dying day I will believe we all thrive when we follow our better instincts.

The way I see it, wisdom isn't just a collection of facts and ideas that you can trot out to then try to make yourself sound smart. Wisdom is when your ideas are embodied and not just in your brain. I believe in being a lifelong learner, but we don't learn things to stick them in a drawer labeled "lessons" and then let them pile up. The whole point of learning things is to put that knowledge to work. Being able to draw on that knowledge is how you're able to find security in your spontaneity.

When a musician sits down and improvises a melody, you might think she's plucking that song miraculously from the air, but that song is the product of thousands of hours of learning to read music, practicing her instrument, and studying what makes a song work. She had to learn the basics before she was qualified to rewrite the rules. Look at Peyton Manning, one of the winningest quarterbacks of all time. He audibled more than nearly any other quarterback of his era. You might call that chutzpah or innate ability, but Manning was famous for spending countless hours studying game tapes and dissecting them for insight. Sure, some of his success has to do with a God-given gift for the game, but you can't discount the lessons he learned and actually put into practice. No doubt he was able to make those calls in a flash on the field because he had taken experience and turned it into opportunity.

Being stupid smart isn't just using what you've learned. It's knowing how to keep your experience from becoming a barrier to new possibilities. There's a difference between experiencing wisdom and being paralyzed by it. Do something enough and you can come down with expert syndrome—the feeling of "I've done this a million times before." That's when complacency sets in, when you rely on your expertise and stop paying attention. You end up missing out on what's new because you are so programmed to see only what you expect to be there. The result is a bad case of confirmation bias, filtering out any information that contradicts what you "know" to be true because, well, it's always been true in the past. That kind of thinking is the surest way to prevent growth.

Think about something you do regularly, something that no longer requires much effort on your part. Now, go back and try to remember the first time you did it. You were curious, open, and engaged. There was the excitement of novelty. You were receptive to possibility. But with repetition, that opening narrows and you let in fewer possibilities. The excitement fades as habits form and doing something well becomes a matter of routine.

What if we could bring that same energy, that same openness we had on our first try, to the thousandth time we do something? I get that it won't feel natural at first. But consider this for a second: every single moment is new. You might have had a similar or almost identical experience in the past, but just by the virtue of time passing, you are different and the world is different. You've never had this experience in this moment.

Life opens up when you bring your experience, but not your expectations, to all that you do. Without all those expectations telling you what you should see, you can take in what is actually there, see it with your own eyes, and process it with your own brain. It's the opposite of cynicism. More "Would you look at that?" than "I know how this is going to go, same old same old" or "I knew that was going to happen." Life is better when we let it surprise us instead of pretending we know what's going to happen.

Life opens up when you bring your experience, but not your expectations, to all that you do. #makesense

Approaching experiences with the enthusiasm of a first-timer instead of the cynicism of an expert can mean setting aside tools that you've relied on for a long time.

Imagine you were on a really long journey, let's say through a desert canyon. You have a big backpack full of tools that have saved your life multiple times. Then, one scalding afternoon you get to a place in the road where the path narrows in the canyon so drastically that you and the backpack can't both make it through. It's too tight. What are you supposed to do? You don't want to leave the backpack behind; its contents have already saved your life countless times. It has been your literal lifeline. But it's either ditch it now or die. There's no way out with all that stuff you're carrying.

You lay the backpack down, and you shimmy through this crack, worried you've just signed your own death sentence. That process is not easy. It's excruciating; it's challenging. It's scarier than you can imagine. Because what if you get through this thing only to find out you need some rope and a pickax, and the rope and pickax are on the other side of the mountain? Still, you continue to shove your butt the rest of the way through. Once you do, there on the other side is an open road where you don't need a rope or an ax. You're now in a completely different situation, a completely different place where the road leading out looks completely different from the road that led in.

Make no mistake: you needed all those tools to a point, but now you're running around free as a bird. Nimble and agile and ready to leap from rock to rock totally unimpeded. You realize you're still you. You didn't get rid of you. You just got rid of the backpack.

That's why I try to hold loosely to my habits and the lessons I've learned: so I can let go of what is no longer serving me well. That way if something new comes along, I'm able to grab it. I can pick up a new skill or tool or lesson that will take me further along in my journey.

I can think of no better example of the benefits of keeping your mind wide-open than parenting. We have five kids, so you'd think we'd know what we are doing by now. We might have a better idea of how to get a two-year-old to eat broccoli or lie down for a nap than we did four kids ago, but with each child it feels like we are learning all over again. And frankly, we are. We get to know each one of these little wonders from scratch, the same way you get to know anyone new in your life. Just because they are our kids doesn't mean they will all respond or act like the one before or after them. We have to take the time to find out what they need and don't need, how they like to communicate, what makes them tick. All of that. It's not a one-size-fits-all deal.

One thing we have learned about being parents is that you can't go through the motions. Kids' needs change constantly, and more importantly, what works for one kid might not work at all for another. For instance, my son Duke has always been a cautious soul. While some little kids might go barreling down the hill on their skateboards or big wheels, Duke was more likely to walk it down and then hop back on at the bottom. When he was young, I'd put him on my shoulders and he'd latch on to my head like a raccoon. It was as if he thought he was one hundred feet in the air.

Because I don't have a cautious bone in my body, there was a time I convinced myself that Duke's careful nature was due to a lack of exposure. When he was just a little guy, I was constantly encouraging him to go for it. It might be *jump off that log, pick up that toad,* or *yell your lungs out!* Back then I thought if I could get him to take a couple of risks, he'd realize how great it felt to throw caution to the wind. I was convinced I was going to be able to teach this kid to have zero fear of heights, maybe even zero fears period. But it just did not take. The boy still prefers to err on the side of safety. Emmie Kay, however—that girl is the first to head toward the high dive just to see how big of a splash she can make.

We've come to realize that each of our kids is unique. Not one of them is a copy of either Jo or me. As parents, we try to see who our kids actually are even if it means setting aside our expectations of who we'd thought or wished they'd be. If one of my kids turns out to be a nine-to-fiver who writes business plans for a living, well, if they love that work and are fulfilled by it, then I wouldn't blink an eye. It's not my thing to force my kids into a predetermined scenario. Besides, it would be a losing battle. You're fighting against nature, against their God-given personality. Life calls Duke to be cautious, and it asks me to take risks. Neither is better; they're just different. That doesn't mean I don't encourage him to take the first step when he's nervous about giving something new a try, but I've definitely realized that it's up to me to learn alongside my kids what they're good at, timid about, and capable of and then mold my parenting style to who they are becoming—not to who I am or who I think they should be.

WHAT FIRES YOU UP?

Nothing gets me hot under the collar like watching people blindly follow the herd instead of following their own hearts, minds, and guts. Maybe for you it's people who act entitled. Or racial inequality. Or the abuse of animals. Or heck, poorly fitting clothes. Instead of suppressing that frustration, get up close and personal with it. Turn that anger into your superpower that spurs you to take action.

What drives you crazy?

What do you find yourself arguing about most passionately?

When does your blood pressure rise?

What does the above suggest about what you're called to do? How can you channel those feelings into a productive purpose?

Which brings me to my next point. Those snap decisions that feel like you're moving effortlessly forward are only possible when you are moving in the direction of your calling.

The word "calling" can sound so lofty. I think of someone who has had a religious experience—they were visited by an angel or saw a burning bush. But I also think it can be simpler than that.

Determining your calling doesn't need to be some elaborate thing where you're hit by lightning and your brain gets rewired. We all have purpose deep inside of us waiting to be discovered. Maybe you don't like the word "calling." Maybe you prefer "passion" or "purpose." Or "vocation," because it's all rolled into one in your life. Either way, I can't tell you what it is. No one can. To paraphrase Frankl again, what life asks of you is different from what it asks of me, or anyone else on the planet.[1] Only you have the answer. Identifying what it is feels like seeing something in the distance and knowing you are already there.

Looking to someone else to show you your purpose would be like you asking me what kind of house design would make you happiest. I can't answer that for you. It depends on you and how you want to live. Almost every single one of our clients tells Jo they want a house where they can entertain because, well, that's what everyone thinks they want. But she is really good at identifying whether that is what they actually want or if they are just regurgitating something they've heard other people say. She'll ask them, "Okay, so tell me about you." And they'll come back talking about their amazing family and how they love to play board games with their kids or watch movies together. That's when Jo will gently point out that maybe a playroom would make more sense for them than a formal dining room. It's all about finding the right purpose for the space. Or for life.

Finding your purpose can be difficult because oftentimes it has been buried under what you think you should be doing instead of what you're actually made to be doing. You get your wires crossed. You copy other people's purposes or cave in to the pressure of what other people expect of you instead of turning to what's inside of you.

You never know what might happen when you let what you feel you're meant to do override what you "should" do.

Take Steve Jobs. He dropped out of Reed College after six months but stuck around campus for a year and a half afterward, sleeping on his friends' floors. Freed from having to worry about taking required courses because he was no longer officially enrolled as a student, Jobs spent his time dropping into classes that caught his interest. At the time, Reed had the premier calligraphy instruction in the nation. Unless you were planning to major in design, there was no reason on earth to take calligraphy. It wasn't going to land you a job at a bank or fulfill your quantitative requirement, but Jobs didn't have a major. He learned what makes beautiful typography simply because it was what he wanted to do.

Fast-forward ten years. Jobs was designing the first Macintosh, which became the first PC with truly beautiful typography, something that sets Apple apart to this day.[2]

Let's investigate your desires for a minute: What do you want? This question has pretty much been trained out of us, but don't hold back or judge yourself. Answer honestly. Maybe you want more time to yourself. Maybe you want to scale back at work so you can spend time with your family. Maybe you want to be a better spouse or a more intentional friend. Maybe you've always wanted to write a novel. Maybe you want to introduce more kindness into the world. Once you identify a yearning, you have a choice. You can give yourself over to the suffering it causes and roll around in the unpleasant feeling of being thwarted or frustrated, or you could listen to what it's telling you. That's how desire creates movement. It's a pull toward something so you can tap into something greater.

I wrote in *Capital Gaines* about how Jo and I work best when we are pulling together in the same direction instead of resisting each other. The analogy I used there was imagining us on the same side of a game of tug-of-war instead of facing off against each other. If I'm pulling one way and she's pulling against me in another, we're both going to be stuck in place. But if we're building strength on strength, we are unstoppable. I think the same thing can be said for following your desires. If you fight who you're meant to be, ignore your deepest desires, try to be someone else, or close yourself off to fresh opportunities, you're going to feel like you're constantly fighting against a strong current of resistance. But if you follow who you *are* meant to be without holding on too tightly to who you *think* you should be or who you have been told to be, there's no limit to how far you can go.

Each and every one of us is irreplaceable. There is something out there that only you can accomplish, that only you were built to do. Nobody else could do it quite the same, even if their life depended on it. What you do ripples through the whole universe, so what opportunities might not open for other people because you aren't doing what you were meant to be doing? What joy or creative thing won't make it into the world if you do not follow your calling? I'm not trying to guilt-trip you; I'm just trying to wake you up to the fact that what you choose to do with your life *matters*.

We are lucky enough to live on a planet populated by people who hold incredible gifts in their hearts. What is your gift—your unique and inimitable gift that gives your life purpose and meaning? What will you do with it?

If you take one thing away from this book, I hope it is this: you must build a network of people around you who can help you answer those questions. God gave each one of us a reason for living. Surround yourself with the people who will help you find and live yours.

At the end of *Capital Gaines* I was on a precipice looking forward with no idea what the future held. All I knew was that Jo and I were turning off a television show—a decision that everybody said was going to bring down all that we had built. But it didn't. We risked everything, but by following our experience, our purpose, and our instincts, by being stupid smart, we've found ourselves in league with opportunities we never could have dreamed. For one thing, we're launching a network that we hope inspires people, that wakes them up, that moves them to want to do something big with their life.

Once again, I don't know what the next chapter holds. Six months from now Magnolia Network could be the biggest failure in the industry's history. But I've taken a chance on people and people have taken a chance on us. Jo and I trusted ourselves to grow, to take risks, to learn, and to trust that kindness and intuition would guide us, that we would be authentic, and that the people in our network would share those values. Whatever the result, I'm happy to die on the sword of "I trusted my network, my gut, and my values to show me the way." Whether we make it or not, there's glory to be had in the journey to the end.

Call it fate, call it chance, call it divine intervention, or simply consider it dumb luck that you picked up this book. Me? I don't believe in coincidences. I believe you were meant for this journey. But I can't take it for you. It's up to you to get up and take that first step toward a life full of the extraordinary. So, how 'bout it? Say goodbye to the status quo, to sleepwalking, to a life set on autopilot, and greet each glorious day with your purpose and passion blazing bright in your heart. There's no time better than this minute, this second, this breath. So let's do this.

Starting.. now.

BOTTOM LINE

There's a lot to be said for expertise, but there's also a lot to be said for keeping an open mind.

CHAPTER 16

WHAT ARE YOU WAITING FOR?

Sixteen is my favorite number—always has been. But this chapter is dedicated to you. Your thoughts, fears, big ideas, and plans for building a network you can count on.

What are you waiting for?

It's time to build this thing:

_____

_____

_____

_____

MAGNOLIA MANIFESTO

We believe in home, that it should restore us from today and ready us for tomorrow. We believe in friendship, because friends who feel like family are the best of friends, and that nothing matters more than family. We believe in seeking the balance between hustle and rest and learning to find contentment in both. We believe everyone deserves a seat at the table and everyone has a story worth telling. We believe in human kindness, knowing we are made better when we all work together. We believe in courage, in cartwheeling past our comfort zones and trying something a little bit scary every day. We believe that failure needn't be a negative thing; rather, we learn from our mistakes and fail smarter next time. We believe in doing good work that matters and, in choosing that, nudging others toward doing the same. We believe that newer isn't always better and that it's time for the pendulum of trend to swing back to the basics. We believe in unearthing beauty, however hidden or subtle it might be. We believe that each day is a gift and that everyday miracles are scattered about if only we have eyes to see. And of all heroic pursuits large or small, we believe there may be none greater than a life well loved.

NOTES

CHAPTER 2: BLUE CHIP

1. Ralph Waldo Emerson, *The Complete Works of Ralph Waldo Emerson*, vol. 8 (New York: Houghton, Mifflin, and Co., 1904), 307, https://books.google.com/books?id=E1WuAAAAIAAJ&pg=PA307.

CHAPTER 3: NONNEGOTIABLES

1. John MacArthur, "Shun What Is Evil," Grace to You, June 11, 2018, https://www.gty.org/library/blog/B180611.

CHAPTER 4: EXTRA-ORDINARY

1. Søren Kierkegaard, *The Sickness unto Death*, ed. and trans. Howard V. Hong and Edna H. Hong (Princeton, NJ: Princeton University Press, 1983), 32–33.

CHAPTER 5: SWERVE

1. Plato, *Republic*, 514a–517a.

CHAPTER 6: UNCOMFORTABLY KIND

1. Architects of Peace Gallery, "Mother Teresa Reflects on Working Toward Peace," Santa Clara University, https://www.scu.edu/mcae/architects-of-peace/Teresa/essay.html.
2. Victor Hugo, *Les Misérables: Complete and Unabridged*, trans. Lee Fahnestock and Norman MacAfee (1987; repr. New York: Signet Classic, 2013), 104.
3. Mark 12:41–44; Luke 21:1–4.

4. Ewan Palmer, "Muslim Political Candidate Helps Pay Off Medical Debt of Man Who Sent Him Islamophobic Tweet," *Newsweek*, March 12, 2020, https://www.newsweek.com/muslim-candidate-qasim-rashid -gofundme-debt-virginia-1491929.

CHAPTER 9: TYING TIES

1. Dale Carnegie, *How to Win Friends and Influence People* (New York: Pocket Books, 1998), 52.
2. Doris Kearns Goodwin, *Team of Rivals: The Political Genius of Abraham Lincoln* (New York: Simon & Schuster, 2006), xv–xvi.
3. Thomas Merton, *No Man Is an Island* (Boston: Mariner Books, 2002), 168.
4. Emmanuel Acho, "Episode 1," *Uncomfortable Conversations with a Black Man*, video, 9:27, June 3, 2020, https://uncomfortableconvos.com /episode/episode-1.
5. Acho, *Uncomfortable Conversations with a Black Man*.
6. Longform, "395: Wesley Lowery," *Longform Podcast*, June 2020, https:// longform.org/posts/longform-podcast-395-wesley-lowery.

CHAPTER 10: INTERACTIONS, NOT TRANSACTIONS

1. *Harry & Meghan: An African Journey*, directed by Nathaniel Lippiett, produced by Natalie Jane Fay, featuring Tom Bradby, Prince Harry, and Meghan Markle, aired October 20, 2019, on ITV, https://www.imdb .com/title/tt11157802/.
2. Isaac Butler, "How to Interview Celebrities, with Taffy Brodesser- Akner," *Slate: Working*, July 12, 2020, https://slate.com/podcasts/working /2020/07/taffy-brodesser-akner-interview-celebrities.

CHAPTER 11: ENGAGE OR ELSE

1. Viktor E. Frankl, *Man's Search for Meaning* (1959; repr., Boston: Beacon Press, 2006), 75.
2. Online Etymology Dictionary, s.v. "intention," https://www.etymonline .com/search?q=intention.
3. Rhitu Chatterjee, "Americans Are a Lonely Lot, and Young People Bear the Heaviest Burden," NPR, May 1, 2018, http://npr.org/sections/health -shots/2018/05/01/606588504/americans-are-a-lonely-lot-and-young -people-bear-the-heaviest-burden.

4. John T. Cacioppo and William Patrick, *Loneliness: Human Nature and the Need for Social Connection* (New York: W. W. Norton, 2009), 31–32.

CHAPTER 12: LET 'EM GROW

1. I changed his name to avoid making him feel uncomfortable if he should ever read this.
2. Gabrielle Hamilton, "My Restaurant Was My Life for 20 Years. Does the World Need It Anymore?" *New York Times Magazine*, updated April 26, 2020, https://www.nytimes.com/2020/04/23/magazine/closing-prune -restaurant-covid.html.
3. Susan Krauss Whitbourne, "Happiness: It's All About the Ending," *Psychology Today*, September 8, 2012, https://www.psychologytoday.com /us/blog/fulfillment-any-age/201209/happiness-it-s-all-about-the -ending.

CHAPTER 13: GREAT(ER) EXPECTATIONS

1. Susan King, "'Alien' at 40: Ridley Scott Explains Why 'You Don't Show the Monster Too Many Times,'" *Variety*, May 24, 2019, https://variety .com/2019/film/news/alien-40-anniverary-ridley-scott-1203223989/.
2. Antoinette McDonald, "04: William Paul Young," *The Beautiful Pursuit*, May 18, 2018, https://thebeautifulpursuit.com/new-blog/2018/5/18 /episode-03-william-paul-young.
3. *Reader's Digest*, September 1947, 64.

CHAPTER 14: FIXER-UPPER MENTALITY

1. Carol Dweck, "Decades of Scientific Research That Started a Growth Mindset Revolution," Mindset Works, https://www.mindsetworks.com /Science/Default.
2. George Bernard Shaw, *Back to Methuselah* (New York: Brentano's, 1921), xiii, https://books.google.com/books?id=ILHdUSvdoEcC&pg=PR13.
3. Bill Bryson, *A Short History of Nearly Everything* (New York: Crown Publishing Group, 2010), 122.
4. Carol S. Dweck, "The Power of Yet," TEDx Talks, published September 12, 2014, YouTube video, 11:18, https://www.youtube.com/watch?v=J -swZaKN2Ic.
5. Timothy D. Wilson et al., "Just Think: The Challenges of the Disengaged Mind," *Science* 345, no. 6192 (July 2014): 75–77.

CHAPTER 15: STUPID SMART

1. Viktor E. Frankl, *Man's Search for Meaning* (1959; repr., Boston: Beacon Press, 2006), 108–9.

2. Steve Jobs, "'You've Got to Find What You Love,' Jobs Says," text of commencement address, Stanford University, June 14, 2005, https://news .stanford.edu/2005/06/14/jobs-061505/.

ABOUT THE AUTHOR

CHIP GAINES is the co-owner and cofounder of Magnolia and a *New York Times* bestselling author of *The Magnolia Story* and *Capital Gaines: Smart Things I Learned Doing Stupid Stuff*. He is constantly reinventing the wheel on what we can achieve together and is always eager to give back to individuals and communities.

Born in Albuquerque and raised in Dallas, Chip later graduated from Baylor University's Hankamer School of Business with a marketing degree. An entrepreneur by nature, Chip has started a number of small businesses and has remodeled hundreds of homes in the Waco area.

But more than any good adventure or hard-working demo day, Chip loves an early morning on the farm and a slow day spent with Jo and their five kids.